Key Element Guide
Service Design

London: TSO

TSO
information & publishing solutions

Published by TSO (The Stationery Office)
and available from:

Online
www.tsoshop.co.uk

Mail, Telephone, Fax & E-mail
TSO
PO Box 29, Norwich NR3 1GN
Telephone orders/General enquiries:
0870 600 5522
Fax orders: 0870 600 5533
E-mail: customer.services@tso.co.uk
Textphone: 0870 240 3701

TSO Shops
16 Arthur Street, Belfast BT1 4GD
028 9023 8451 Fax 028 9023 5401
71 Lothian Road, Edinburgh EH3 9AZ
0870 606 5566 Fax 0870 606 5588

TSO@Blackwell and other Accredited Agents

Published with the permission of the Office of
Government Commerce on behalf of the Controller
of Her Majesty's Stationery Office

© Crown Copyright 2008

This is a Crown copyright value added product, reuse
of which requires a Click-Use Licence for value added
material issued by OPSI.

Applications to reuse, reproduce or republish
material in this publication should be sent to OPSI,
Information Policy Team, St Clements House, 2-16
Colegate, Norwich, NR3 1BQ, Tel No (01603) 621000
Fax No (01603) 723000, E-mail: hmsolicensing@
cabinet-office.x.gsi.gov.uk , or complete the
application form on the OPSI website http://www.
opsi.gov.uk/click-use/value-added-licence-
information/index.htm

OPSI, in consultation with Office of Government
Commerce (OGC), may then prepare a Value Added
Licence based on standard terms tailored to your
particular requirements including payment terms

The OGC logo® is a Registered Trade Mark of the
Office of Government Commerce in the United
Kingdom

ITIL® is a Registered Trade Mark of the Office of
Government Commerce in the United Kingdom and
other countries

The Swirl logo™ is a Trade Mark of the Office of
Government Commerce

First published 2008

ISBN 9780113310715 (Sold in a pack of 10 copies)
ISBN 9780113311200 (Single copy ISBN)

Printed in the United Kingdom for The Stationery
Office
N5745153   03/08

Contents

Acknowledgements

ITIL AUTHORING TEAM

- Sharon Taylor (Aspect Group Inc.) Chief Architect
- Vernon Lloyd (Fox IT) Author
- Colin Rudd (ITEMS) Author

REVIEWERS

OGC would like to recognize the contribution of the following individuals:

Alison Cartlidge, Deirdre Conniss, Robert Falkowitz, Matiss Horodishtiano, Chris Jones, Stuart Rance, Siegfried Schmitt, Dean Taylor and Cheryl Tovizi

and from *it*SMF's International Publications Executive Sub-Committee (IPESC):

Matiss Horodishtiano (Lead Assessor), Jorge Aballay (Argentina), Marianna Billington (NZ), Bart van Brabant (Belgium), Peter Brooks (SA), Jenny Ellwood-Wade (NZ), Ashley Hanna (UK), Signe Marie Hernes (Norway), Sergio Hrabinski (Argentina), Robert Stroud (US) and Wilfred Wah (Hong Kong).

1 Introduction

This publication is intended to provide a synopsis of the basic concepts and practice elements of Service Design, which forms part of the core ITIL Service Management Practices. These practices form the ITIL Service Lifecycle on which the concepts of these and all other ITIL Service Management publications are based.

This publication is not intended to replace the ITIL core publications and should not be used in place of the full practice guidance publications. The content in this publication is depicted at a high level and will not be practical as a substitute for the full guidance publication; rather it should serve as a handy quick reference that is portable and helps direct the reader to the full guidance information when needed.

1.1 THE ITIL FRAMEWORK

ITIL Service Management has been practised successfully around the world for more than 20 years. Over this time, the framework has evolved from a specialized set of service management topics with a focus on function to a process-based framework and now to a broader, holistic service lifecycle. The evolution and transformation of ITIL Service Management Practices is the result of the evolution of the IT service management (ITSM) industry itself, through knowledge, experience, technical innovation and thought leadership. The ITIL Service Lifecycle is both a reflection of the industry practice in use today, and concepts that will move us forward in the future of service management philosophies and practices.

The objective of the ITIL Service Management Practices framework is to provide services to business customers that are fit for purpose, stable and which are so reliable that business views them as a trusted utility.

ITIL Service Management Practices offer best-practice guidance applicable to all types of organizations that provide services to a business. Each publication addresses capabilities having direct impact on a service provider's performance. The structure of the core practice takes form in a service lifecycle. It is iterative and multidimensional. It ensures organizations are set up to leverage capabilities in one area for learning and improvements in others. The core is expected to provide structure, stability and strength to service management capabilities with durable principles, methods and tools. This serves to protect investments and provide the necessary basis for measurement, learning and improvement.

The guidance in the ITIL framework can be adapted for use in various business environments and organizational strategies. The complementary guidance provides flexibility to implement the core in a diverse range of environments. Practitioners can select complementary guidance as needed to provide traction for the core in a given business context, in much the same way as tyres are selected based on the type of automobile, purpose and road conditions. This is to increase the durability and portability of knowledge assets and to protect investments in service management capabilities.

1.2 THE ITIL CORE PRACTICE PUBLICATIONS

The ITIL Service Management Practices comprise three main sets of products and services:

- Core guidance
- Complementary guidance
- Web support services.

1.2.1 ITIL Service Management Practices – core guidance

The core set consists of six publications:

- *The Official Introduction to the ITIL Service Lifecycle*
- *Service Strategy*
- *Service Design*
- *Service Transition*
- *Service Operation*
- *Continual Service Improvement*.

A common structure across all the core guidance publications helps the reader to find references between volumes and to know where to look for similar guidance topics within each stage of the lifecycle.

1.2.2 ITIL Service Management Practices – complementary guidance

This is a living library of publications with guidance specific to industry sectors, organization types, operating models and technology architectures. Each publication supports and enhances the guidance in the ITIL Service Management core. Publications in this category will be continually added to the complementary guidance library and will contain contributions from the expert and user ITSM community. In this way, ITIL Service Management Practices are illustrated in real-life situations and in a variety of contexts that add value and knowledge to your own ITIL practice.

1.2.3 ITIL Service Management Practices – web support services

These products are online, interactive services, which will develop over time and include elements such as the glossary of terms and definitions, the interactive service model, online subscriber services, case studies, templates and ITIL Live® – an interactive expert knowledge centre where users can access time with ITSM experts to discuss questions and issues, and seek advice.

Readers of this key element guide are encouraged to explore the entire portfolio of ITIL Service Management publications and services.

1.3 WHAT IS A SERVICE?

Service management is more than just a set of capabilities. It is also a professional practice supported by an extensive body of knowledge, experience and skills. A global community of individuals and organizations in the public and private sectors fosters its growth and maturity. Formal schemes exist for the education, training and certification of practising organizations, and individuals influence its quality. Industry best practices, academic research and formal standards contribute to its intellectual capital and draw from it.

Definition of a service
A service is a means of delivering value to customers by facilitating outcomes customers want to achieve without the ownership of specific costs and risks.

1.4 WHAT IS A LIFECYCLE?

The service lifecycle contains five elements, each of which relies on service principles, processes, roles and performance measures. The ITIL Service Lifecycle uses a hub and spoke design, with Service Strategy at the hub, and Service Design, Transition and Operation as the revolving lifecycle stages, anchored by Continual Service Improvement (Figure 1.1). Each part of the lifecycle exerts influence on the others and relies on the others for inputs and feedback. In this way, a constant set of checks and balances throughout the service lifecycle ensures that as business demand changes with business need, the services can adapt and respond effectively to them.

Figure 1.1 The ITIL Service Lifecycle

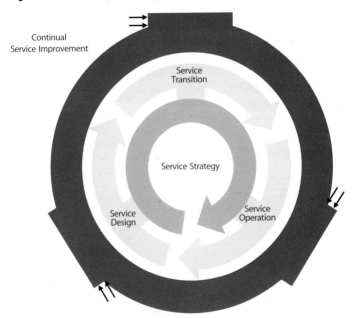

At the heart of the service lifecycle is the key principle – all services must provide measurable value to business objectives and outcomes. ITIL Service Management focuses on business value as its prime objective. Each practice revolves around ensuring that everything a service provider does to manage IT services for the business customer can be measured and quantified in terms of business value. This has become extremely important of late as IT organizations are required to operate as businesses in order to demonstrate a clear return on investment, equating service performance with business value to the customer.

2 The ITIL Service Management Model

The ITIL Service Lifecycle uses models to refine and customize an organization's use of the ITIL Service Management Practices. These models are intended to be reusable in a variety of organizational contexts and to help take advantage of economies of scale and efficiencies.

Central to these models are the overarching process elements that interact throughout the lifecycle and bring power and wisdom to service practices. These service model process elements consist of two main types – lifecycle governance and lifecycle operations. These are depicted in Figure 2.1.

Figure 2.1 Process elements of the ITIL Service Lifecycle

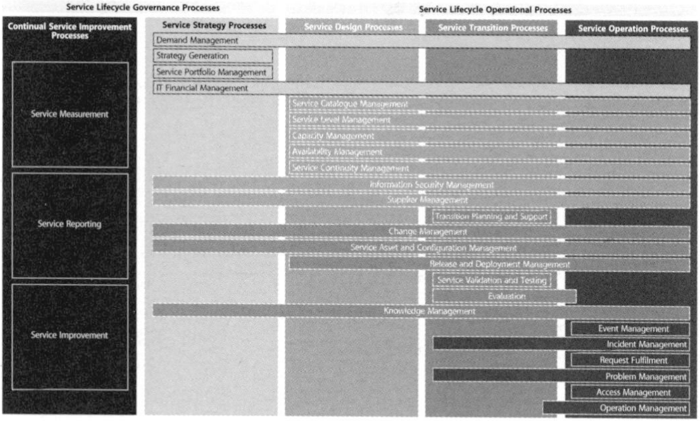

While these processes are non-linear, they do have a logical and sometimes sequential flow. To illustrate this, Figure 2.2 shows the high-level, basic flow of lifecycle process elements in the ITIL Service Lifecycle.

Figure 2.2 A high-level view of the ITIL Service Management Model

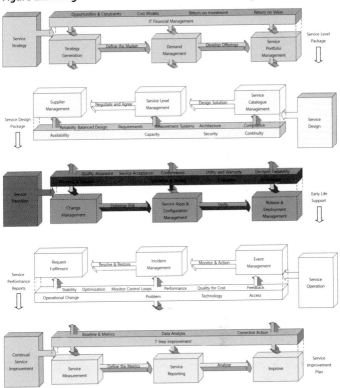

This publication deals with the high-level concepts drawn from the Service Design stage of the service lifecycle.

3   Principles of Service Design

Great services do not exist by accident. They have to be carefully planned and designed. Service Design is the means to achieve this. The best Service Strategy cannot be realized without well-designed services. Effective Service Design can lead organizations to greater gains in quality and cost-effectiveness. It reduces the risk of costly compensating for design flaws in the operational environment, and ensures that services will perform as they are intended and bring measurable value to the business objectives.

The Service Design phase of the ITIL Service Lifecycle takes business requirements and, using five aspects for Service Design, creates services and their supporting practices, which meet business demands for quality, reliability and flexibility. Service Design is iterative throughout the Service Lifecycle, and begins with a solid blueprint that enables the build, test and release stages of Service Transition through the Service Design Package (SDP).

The primary objective of Service Management is to ensure that the IT services are aligned to the business needs and actively support them. It is imperative that the IT services underpin the business processes, and it is also increasingly important that IT acts as an agent for change to facilitate business transformation.

Most authorities now identify four types of IT assets that need to be acquired and managed in order to contribute to effective IT service provision. These are IT infrastructure, applications, information and people. Specifically there is a strong emphasis on the acquisition, management and integration of these assets throughout their 'birth to retirement' lifecycle. The delivery of quality IT services depends on the effective and efficient management of these assets. These assets on their own, however, are not enough to meet the Service Management needs of the business. ITIL Service Management practices use these four asset types as part of a set of capabilities and resources called 'service assets'.

The context of this publication is the ITIL Framework as a source of good practice in Service Management. ITIL Service Management Practices are used by organizations worldwide to establish and improve capabilities in Service Management. ISO/IEC 20000 provides a formal and universal standard for organizations seeking to have their Service Management capabilities audited and certified. The ITIL core consists of six publications. Each provides the guidance necessary for an integrated approach, as required by the ISO/IEC 20000 standard.

3.1 KEY ELEMENTS

The main purpose of the Service Design stage of the lifecycle is the design of new or changed services. It is important to adopt a holistic approach to all five aspects of Service Design to ensure consistency and integration within all activities and processes across the entire IT technology, providing end-to-end business-related functionality, management and quality. It is also important that when changing or amending any of the individual elements of design, all the other aspects are considered.

Not every change within an IT service requires the instigation of Service Design activity. It is only required where there is 'significant' change. However, each organization must define what constitutes 'significant', so that everyone is clear as to when Service Design activity is required.

The Service Design stage of the lifecycle starts with a set of new or changed business requirements and ends with the development of a service solution designed to meet the documented needs of the business. This developed solution, together with its SDP, is then passed to Service Transition to evaluate, build, test and deploy the new or changed service. Figure 3.1 shows the overall scope of Service Design, the key processes involved and the five aspects of design and how they interact.

Figure 3.1 Scope of Service Design

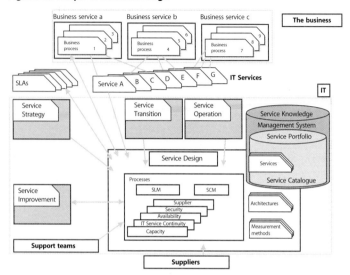

As stated above, the main aim of Service Design is the design of new or changed services. The requirements for these new services are extracted from the Service Portfolio. Each requirement is analysed, documented and agreed, and a solution design is produced that is then compared with the strategies and constraints from Service Strategy to ensure that it conforms to corporate and IT policies. Each individual Service Design is also considered in conjunction with each of the other four aspects of Service Design.

The implementation of ITIL Service Management is about preparing and planning the effective and efficient use of the four Ps: the People, the Processes, the Products (services, technology and tools) and the Partners (suppliers, manufacturers and vendors) (Figure 3.2).

Figure 3.2 The four Ps

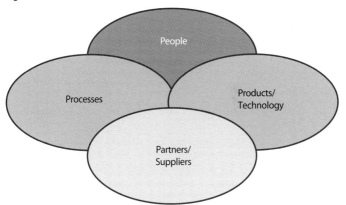

In order to ensure that business and IT services remain synchronized, many organizations form committees of senior management from the business and IT organizations. This committee carries the overall accountability for setting governance, direction, priority, policy and strategy for IT services. Many organizations refer to this group as the IT Strategy or Steering Group (ISG). The role of an ISG is to act as a partnership between IT and the business. It should meet regularly to review the business and IT strategies, designs, plans, architectures and policies to ensure close alignment. ISG has an important role in the alignment of business and IT strategies, and the Service Portfolio is a key source of input to the ISG in its decision-making role.

The optimizing of design activities requires the implementation of documented processes, together with an overriding quality management system (QMS), such as ISO 9001, for their continual measurement and improvement. The impact on all stages of the lifecycle should be measured and not just the impact on the design stage. Therefore, the measurements and metrics should look at the amount of rework and improvement activity needed on transition, operation and improvement as a result of design issues.

When designing a service or a process, it is imperative that all the roles are clearly defined. A trademark of high-performing organizations is the ability to make the right decisions quickly and execute them effectively.

3.2 THE SERVICE DESIGN PRACTICE

A new application should not be designed and developed in isolation. As stated in section 3.1, individual elements of design should be amended or changed using a holistic approach that considers all the other aspects of design, that is, the impact on the overall service, the management systems and tools (e.g. Service Portfolio and Service Catalogue), the architectures, the technology, the Service Management processes and the necessary measurements and metrics. This will ensure not only that the functional elements are addressed by the design, but also that all of the management and operational requirements are addressed as a fundamental part of the design and are not added as an afterthought.

Five individual aspects of Service Design are covered in this publication. These are the design of:

- **New or changed services** – the design of new or changed services is the main aim of Service Design. Each service solution is considered in conjunction with the other four aspects of Service Design
- **The Service Management systems and tools, especially the Service Portfolio** – to ensure that this new or changed service is consistent with all other services

- **The technology architectures and management systems** – to ensure that all the technology architectures and management systems are consistent and can manage the new service
- **The processes** – to ensure that the processes, roles, responsibilities and skills can operate, support and maintain the new or changed service
- **The measurement methods and metrics** – to ensure that they can provide the required metrics on the new or changed service.

The key processes elements within the design phase of the Service Lifecycle are:

- **Service Catalogue Management** – to ensure a Service Catalogue is maintained, containing accurate information on all operational services
- **Service Level Management (SLM)** – negotiates and agrees service targets with the business, and then produces reports on the service provider's ability to deliver agreed levels of service
- **Capacity Management** – ensures cost-justifiable IT capacity in all areas of IT exists and is matched to the current and future agreed needs of the business
- **Availability Management (AM)** – ensures the level of service availability in all services is matched to, or exceeds, the agreed needs of the business
- **IT Service Continuity Management (ITSCM)** – ensures the required IT and service facilities can be resumed within required, and agreed, business timescales
- **Information Security Management** – aligns IT security with business security, and ensures effective management of security in all activities and services
- **Supplier Management** – manages suppliers and the services they supply to provide seamless quality of IT service to the business.

IT Service Design is a part of the overall business change process. Figure 3.3 illustrates this business change process and the role of IT.

Figure 3.3 The business change process

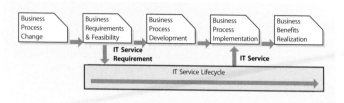

The role of the Service Design stage within this overall business change process can be defined as:

> 'The design of appropriate and innovative IT services, including their architectures, processes, policies and documentation, to meet current and future agreed business requirements.'

It is important that the right interfaces and links to the design activities exist. When designing new or changed services, it is vital that all aspects of the business, the service, the entire Service Lifecycle and ITSM processes are involved from the outset. Often difficulties occur in operations when a newly designed service is handed over for live running at the last minute. The composition of a service and its constituent parts is illustrated in Figure 3.4.

Figure 3.4 Service composition

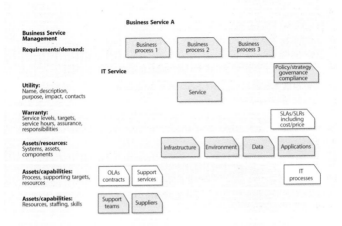

The design activities must not consider each of the components in Figure 3.4 in isolation; rather they must also consider the relationships between each of the components and their interactions and dependencies on any other components and services, in order to provide an effective and comprehensive solution that meets the business needs.

The main goals and objectives of Service Design are to:

- Design services to satisfy business objectives
- Design services that can be easily and efficiently developed and enhanced
- Design efficient and effective processes for high-quality IT services
- Identify and manage risks so that they can be removed or mitigated
- Design secure and resilient technologies, resources and capability

- Design measurement methods and metrics for assessing process effectiveness and efficiency
- Produce and maintain IT plans, processes, policies, architectures, frameworks and documents
- Develop IT skills and capability by moving strategy and design into operational activities
- Contribute to the improvement of the overall quality of IT.

For any new business requirements, the design of services is a delicate balancing act, ensuring that not only the functional requirements but also the performance targets are met. This all needs to be balanced with regard to the resources available within the required timescale and the costs of the new services.

Service Design must consider all elements of the service by taking a holistic approach to the design of a new service. This approach should consider the service and its constituent components and their inter-relationships, ensuring that the services delivered meet the functionality and quality of service expected by the business in all areas. Figure 3.5 illustrates the relationships and dependencies between these elements.

The key Service Design activities are:

- Business requirements collection, analysis and engineering to ensure they are clearly documented
- Design of appropriate services, technology, processes, information and measurements
- Production and revision of all design processes and documents involved in Service Design
- Liaison with all other design and planning activities and roles, e.g. solution design
- Production and maintenance of IT policies and design documents, including designs, plans, architectures and policies
- Risk assessment and management of all services, design processes and deliverables
- Ensuring alignment with all corporate and IT strategies and policies.

Figure 3.5 The service relationships and dependencies

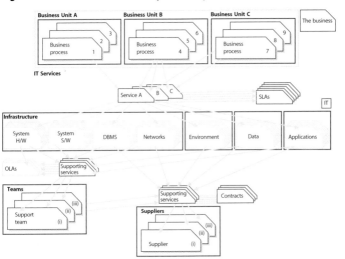

The inputs to the various design activities include corporate and business strategies, objectives, policies and plans, constraints and compliance requirements, all IT strategies, policies and plans, financial budgets and plans, together with all Service Management strategies, policies, objectives and plans (especially the Service Portfolio).

The inputs to the various design activities are:

■ All corporate and business strategies and strategic documents and plans
■ Constraints and requirements for compliance with legislated standards and regulations

- All IT strategies and strategic documents and plans, including the Service Portfolio
- Measurements and measurement tools and techniques.

The deliverables from the design activities are:

- Suggested revisions to IT strategies and policies
- Revised designs, plans and technology and management architectures
- Designs for new or changed services, processes and technologies
- Process review and analysis reports, with revised and improved processes and procedures
- Revised measurement methods and processes
- Managed levels of risk, and risk assessment and management reports
- Business cases and feasibility studies, together with statements of requirements (SORs) and invitations to tender (ITTs)
- Business benefit and realization reviews, reports and feedback on all other plans.

3.3   THE FIVE DESIGN ASPECTS

3.3.1   Designing service solutions

The key aspect is the design of new or changed service solutions to meet changing business needs. Every time a new service solution is produced, it needs to be checked against each of the other four aspects to ensure that it will integrate and interface with all of the other services already in existence. The plans produced by Service Design for the design, transition and subsequent operation of new service solutions should include:

- The approach taken and the associated timescales
- The organizational impact of the new solution on the business and IT
- The commercial impact of the solution on the organization
- The technical impact of the solution and the people

- The commercial justification assessment of the impact of the solution
- The assessment and mitigation of risks to services, processes and activities
- Communication planning and all aspects of communication with all parties
- The impact of the solution on new or existing contracts or agreements
- The expected outcomes from the operation of the new or changed service
- The production of an SDP
- The production of a set of Service Acceptance Criteria.

The most effective way of managing all aspects of services through their lifecycle is by using appropriate management systems and tools to support and automate efficient processes. The Service Portfolio (Figure 3.6) is the most critical management system used to support all processes and describes a provider's services in terms of business value. It articulates business needs and the provider's response to those needs. By definition, business value terms correspond to market terms, providing a means for comparing service competitiveness across alternative providers. By acting as the basis of a decision framework, a Service Portfolio forms the spine of a comprehensive Service Knowledge Management System (SKMS).

3.3.2 Designing supporting systems

Once a strategic decision to charter a service is made, this is the stage in the Service Lifecycle when Service Design begins architecting the service, which will eventually become part of the Service Catalogue. The Service Portfolio should contain information relating to every service and its current status within the organization. It is the main source of information on the requirements and services, and must be very carefully designed to ensure that it meets the needs of all of its users. The design should be approached in the same way as the design of any other IT service or Service Management information system.

Figure 3.6 The Service Portfolio – a central repository

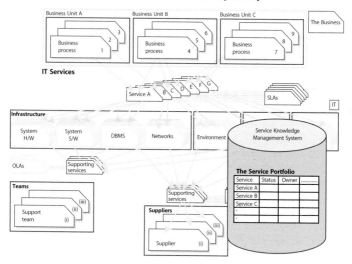

3.3.3 Designing technology architectures

The architectural design activities within an IT organization are concerned with providing the overall strategic 'blueprints' for the development and deployment of an IT infrastructure – a set of applications and data that satisfy the current and future needs of the business. Although these aspects underpin the delivery of quality IT services, they alone cannot deliver quality IT services, and it is essential that the people, process and partner aspects are also considered.

Definition of architectural design

The development and maintenance of IT policies, strategies, architectures, designs, documents, plans and processes for the deployment and subsequent operation and improvement of appropriate IT services and solutions throughout an organization.

An Enterprise Architecture should show how all elements are integrated in order to achieve the business objectives, both now and in the future. The complete Enterprise Architecture can be large and complex. Here we are interested in those architectures concerned with the business of the organization and the information systems that support it. The Enterprise Architecture should be an integrated element of the Business Architecture and should include the following major areas:

- **Service Architecture** – which translates applications, infrastructure, organization and support activities into a set of services
- **Application Architecture** – which provides a blueprint for the development and deployment of individual applications and maps links between business processes and applications
- **Data/Information Architecture** – which describes the logical and physical data assets of the enterprise and the data management resources
- **IT Infrastructure Architecture** – which describes the structure, functionality and geographical distribution of the hardware, software and communications components
- **Environmental Architecture** – which describes all aspects, types and levels of environment controls and their management.

The development, documentation and maintenance of business and IT architectures will typically form part of the processes of strategic thinking and strategy development within an organization (Figure 3.7).

Figure 3.7 Architectural relationships

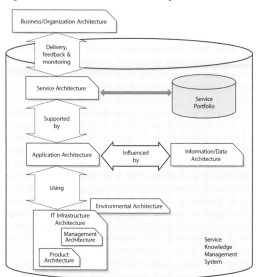

Within the framework described earlier, it is possible to identify (at least) three architectural roles. These could all report to a senior 'Enterprise Architect' in the organization:

- **Business/Organizational Architect** – concerned with business models and business processes
- **Service Architect** – concerned with the Service, Data and Application Architectures

- **IT Infrastructure Architect** – concerned with the physical technology model.

If the necessary architectures are in place, Service Design:

- Must work within the agreed architectural framework and standards
- Will be able to re-use many of the assets created as part of the architecture
- Should work closely with all architectural roles to ensure maximum benefit from the architectures.

3.3.4 Designing processes

A process is a structured set of activities designed to accomplish a specific objective. A process takes one or more inputs and turns them into defined outputs. A process includes all of the roles, responsibilities, tools and management controls required to reliably deliver the outputs. A process may also define or revise policies, standards, guidelines, activities, processes, procedures and work instructions if they are needed.

Definition of process control

The activity of planning and regulating a process, with the objective of performing a process in an effective, efficient and consistent manner.

Processes, once defined, should be documented and controlled. Once under control, they can be repeated and become manageable. Degrees of control over processes can be defined, and then process measurement and metrics can be built into the process to control and improve the process (Figure 3.8).

Figure 3.8 The generic process elements

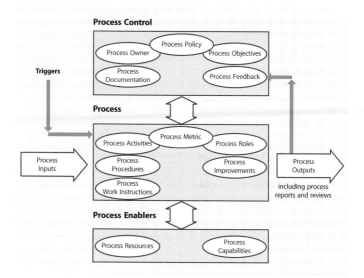

The generic process elements show data enters the process, is processed, is output and the outcome is measured and reviewed. This very basic description underpins any process description. A process is always organized around a set of objectives. The main outputs from the process should be driven by the objectives, and should always include process measurements (metrics), reports and process improvement.

Each process should be owned by a Process Owner, who should be responsible for the process and its improvement and for ensuring that a process meets its objectives. The objectives of any IT process should be defined in measurable terms and should be expressed in terms of business benefits and underpinning business strategy and goals. Service Design should assist each Process Owner with the design of processes to ensure that all processes use standard terms and templates, are consistent and integrate with each other to provide end-to-end integration across all areas.

3.3.5 Design of measurement systems and metrics

In order to manage and control the design processes, they have to be monitored and measured. This is true for all aspects of the design processes. Care should be exercised when selecting measurements, metrics and the methods used to produce them, because the metrics and measurements chosen will actually affect and change the behaviour of people working within the activities and processes being measured, particularly where this relates to objectives, and personal and team performance. Therefore, only measurements that encourage progression towards business objectives or desired behavioural change should be selected.

In all the design activities, the requirement should be to:

- Design solutions that are 'fit for purpose'
- Design for the appropriate level of quality – not over-engineered or under-engineered
- Design solutions that are 'right first time' and meet their expected targets
- Design solutions that minimize the amount of 'rework' or 'add-ons' that are subsequently required
- Design effective and efficient solutions from the perspective of the business and the customers.

Measurement methods and metrics should reflect these requirements and all measurements and metrics used should reflect the quality and success of the processes from the perspective of the business and the customers and users. They need to reflect the ability of the delivered solutions to meet the identified and agreed requirements of the business. The process measurements selected need to be appropriate to the capability and maturity of the processes being measured.

Immature processes are not capable of supporting sophisticated measurements and methods. There are four types of metrics that can be used to measure the capability and performance of processes:

- **Progress** – milestones and deliverables in the capability of the process
- **Compliance** – compliance of the process to governance requirements, regulatory requirements and compliance of people to the process
- **Effectiveness** – the accuracy and correctness of the process and its ability to deliver the 'right result'
- **Efficiency** – the productivity of the process, its speed, throughput and resource utilization.

The primary metrics should always focus on determining the effectiveness and the quality of the solutions provided. Secondary metrics can then measure the efficiency of the processes used to produce and manage the solution. The priority should always be to ensure that the processes provide the correct results for the business. Therefore, the measurement methods and metrics should always provide this business-focused measurement above all. The most effective method of measurement is to establish a 'Metrics Tree' or 'KPI tree'. Too many organizations collect measurements in individual areas, but fail to aggregate them together to gain the full benefit of the measurements, and therefore suffer.

Therefore, organizations should use automated measurement systems in the form of a 'Metrics Tree' (Figure 3.9).

Figure 3.9 The Metrics Tree

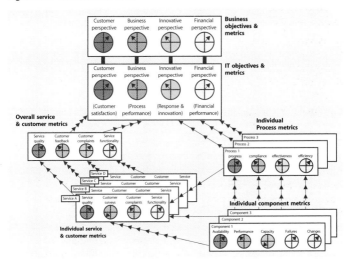

Figure 3.9 is illustrative of an example of a Metrics Tree based on a typical Balanced Scorecard. Balanced Scorecards represent a management system that enables increasing numbers of organizations to clarify their vision and strategy into action. They provide feedback regarding the internal business processes and external outcomes, in order continually to improve strategic performance and results. This enables everybody within the organization to get a picture of the performance of the organization at the appropriate level:

- Business managers and customers can get a 'top-level' business 'dashboard', aligned with business needs and processes
- Senior IT managers and customers can focus on the top-level IT management 'dashboard'

- Service Managers and customers can focus on the performance of particular services
- Process Owners and managers can view the performance of their processes
- Technical specialists can look at the performance of individual components
- The dashboard also presents an opportunity to view trends over time, rather than static data, so that potential performance degradation can be identified and rectified at an early stage.

3.4 DESIGN CONSTRAINTS

All design activities operate within many constraints. These constraints come from the business and Service Strategy and cover many different areas (Figure 3.10).

Figure 3.10 Design constraints driven by strategy

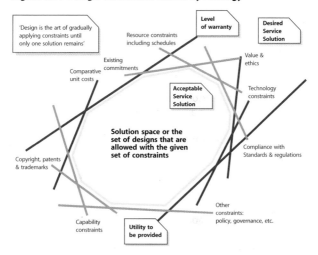

This means that designers are not always 'free' to design the most appropriate solution for the business, because the design does not fall within the imposed constraints, as illustrated previously. The designer can only provide the solution that fits within all of the currently known constraints, or else try lifting or renegotiating some of the constraints. External influences impose additional constraints, such as the need for good corporate and IT governance and compliance with legislation and standards.

3.5 ROLES AND RESPONSIBILITIES

For Service Design to be successful, it is essential to define the roles and responsibilities of the various activities within the organization. When designing a service or a process, it is imperative that all the roles are clearly defined. A trademark of high-performing organizations is the ability to make the right decisions quickly and execute them effectively. Whether the decision involves a strategic choice or a critical operation, being clear about who has input, who decides and who takes action will enable the company to move forward rapidly.

The RACI model will be beneficial in enabling decisions to be made with pace and confidence. RACI is an acronym for the four main roles of:

- **Responsible** – the person or people responsible for getting the job done
- **Accountable** – only one person can be accountable for each task
- **Consulted** – the people who are consulted and whose opinions are sought
- **Informed** – the people who are kept up-to-date on progress.

Occasionally, an expanded version of RACI is used, called RACI-VS, with two more roles as follows:

- **Verifies** – the person or group that checks whether the acceptance criteria have been met
- **Signs off** – the person who approves the V decision and authorizes the product hand-off.

3.5.1 Skills and attributes

The specific roles within ITIL Service Management all require specific skills, attributes and competences from the people involved to enable them to work effectively and efficiently. However, whatever the role, it is imperative that the person carrying out that role has good general attributes, including business and customer skills, technology skills, management skills and communications skills. More information about the skills and competences of these roles can be found within the Skills Framework for the Information Age (SFIA) – see www.sfia.org.uk.

The following are illustrations of the main activities within each of the Service Design roles.

Process Owner

A Process Owner is responsible for ensuring that their process is being performed according to the agreed and documented process, and is meeting the aims of the process definition.

Service Design Manager

The key role and responsibilities of the Service Design Manager are covered throughout this publication. The Service Design Manager is responsible for the overall coordination and deployment of quality solution designs for services and processes.

IT Designer/Architect

An IT Designer/Architect:

■ Is responsible for the overall coordination and design of the required technology
■ Understands how architectures, strategies, designs and plans fit together
■ Understands all the main aspects of design
■ Produces a detailed process map that documents all the processes and their high-level interfaces.

Service Catalogue Manager

The Service Catalogue Manager has responsibility for producing and maintaining an accurate Service Catalogue. The activities associated with this role include ensuring that:

- All operational services and all services being prepared for operational running are recorded within the Service Catalogue
- All the information within the Service Catalogue is accurate and up-to-date
- The Service Catalogue is consistent with the information within the Service Portfolio
- The information within the Service Catalogue is adequately protected and backed up.

Service Level Manager

The Service Level Manager has responsibility for ensuring that the aims of SLM are met. The main activities associated with this role are:

- Keeping aware of changing business needs, ensuring that the current and future service requirements of customers are identified, understood and documented in Service Level Agreements (SLAs) and Service Level Reports (SLRs)
- Negotiating and agreeing levels of service to be delivered with the customer (either internal or external); formally documenting these levels of service in SLAs
- Negotiating and agreeing Operational Level Agreements (OLAs) and, in some cases, other SLAs, contracts and agreements that underpin the SLAs with the customers of the service
- Assisting with the production and maintenance of an accurate Service Portfolio, Service Catalogue, Application Portfolio and the corresponding maintenance procedures
- Ensuring that service reports are produced for each customer service and that breaches of SLA targets are highlighted, investigated and actions taken to prevent their recurrence

- Ensuring that SLA, and service scope and performance reviews are scheduled, carried out with customers regularly and are documented with agreed actions progressed
- Ensuring that improvement initiatives identified in service reviews are acted on and progress reports are provided to customers
- Identifying and developing relationships with all key stakeholders and customers
- Defining and agreeing complaints and their recording, management, escalation, where necessary, and resolution
- Measuring, recording, analysing and improving customer satisfaction, including management of complaints and compliments.

Availability Manager

The Availability Manager has responsibility for ensuring that the aims of AM are met. The main activities associated with this role are:

- Ensuring that existing services deliver the levels of availability agreed with the business in SLAs
- Ensuring that all new services are designed to deliver the levels of availability required by the business, and validation of the final service design
- Assisting with the investigation and diagnosis of all Incidents and Problems that cause availability issues or unavailability of services or components
- Participating in IT infrastructure design, specifying component availability requirements
- Reviewing and improving the Availability Management Information System (AMIS) and availability event management systems
- Specifying the reliability, maintainability and serviceability requirements for components supplied by internal and external suppliers
- Monitoring IT availability achieved against SLA targets, and providing a range of IT availability, reliability and maintainability reporting to ensure that agreed levels of availability are measured
- Proactively improving and optimizing service availability wherever possible

- Regularly reviewing the AM process, and its associated techniques and methods
- Creating availability and recovery design criteria to be applied to new or enhanced designs
- Maintaining and completing an availability testing schedule for all availability mechanisms.

IT Service Continuity Manager

The IT Service Continuity Manager is responsible for ensuring that the aims of ITSCM are met, including the following key activities:

- Performing Business Impact Analyses for all existing and new services
- Implementing and maintaining the ITSCM process, in accordance with the overall requirements of the organization's Business Continuity Management (BCM) process
- Ensuring that all ITSCM plans, risks and activities underpin and align with all BCM plans, risks and activities, and are capable of meeting the agreed targets under any circumstances
- Performing risk assessment and risk management to prevent disasters where cost-justifiable
- Developing and maintaining the organization's continuity strategy and ITSCM plans
- Assessing potential service continuity issues and invoking Service Continuity Plans if necessary
- Managing Service Continuity Plans while in operation
- Performing post-mortem reviews of service continuity tests and invocations, and instigating corrective actions where required
- Maintaining an IT testing schedule, including testing all plans in line with business needs
- Communicating and maintaining awareness of ITSCM objectives within the business areas
- Undertaking regular reviews, at least annually, of the Continuity Plans with the business areas to ensure that they accurately reflect the business needs.

Capacity Manager

The Capacity Manager has responsibility for ensuring that the aims of Capacity Management are met, by performing the following key activities:

- Ensuring that there is adequate IT capacity to meet required levels of service, and that capacity is matched to agreed and future demand
- Identifying, capacity requirements through discussions with the business users and SLM
- Understanding and using the maximum and current usage of infrastructure and services
- Forecasting future capacity requirements based on business plans, usage trends, new services etc., and performing sizing on proposed new services, possibly using modelling techniques
- Production, regular review and revision of the Capacity Plan, in line with the organization's business planning cycle, identifying usage and forecasts during the period covered by the plan
- Ensuring that appropriate levels of monitoring of resources and system performance are set
- Analysis of usage and performance data, reporting on performance against SLA targets, current usage, trends and forecasts
- Identifying and initiating any tuning to optimize and improve capacity or performance
- Assessing new technology and techniques and their relevance to the business and service designs
- Producing management reports that include current usage of resources, trends and forecasts.

Security Manager

The Security Manager is responsible for performing the following activities to ensure that the aims of Information Security Management (ISM) are met:

- Developing and maintaining the Information Security policy and a supporting set of policies
- Ensuring that the Information Security policy is enforced and communicated to all parties

- Identifying and classifying IT assets and the level of control and protection required
- Assisting with Business Impact Analyses
- Performing Security Risk Analysis and risk management, designing and maintaining appropriate security controls and security plans with procedures for their operation and maintenance
- Maintaining a set of security controls and documentation, and regularly reviewing all procedures
- Monitoring and managing all security breaches, taking remedial action to prevent recurrence
- Reporting, analysing and reducing the impact and volumes of all security Incidents
- Performing regular and ad hoc security tests
- Ensuring that the confidentiality, integrity and availability of the services are maintained
- Ensuring that all access to services by external partners and suppliers is subject to contractual agreements and responsibilities.

Supplier Manager

The Supplier Manager has responsibility for ensuring that the aims of Supplier Management are met, by completing the following main activities:

- Providing assistance in the development and review of SLAs, contracts and agreements with suppliers
- Ensuring that value for money is obtained from all IT suppliers and contracts
- Ensuring that all IT supplier processes are consistent and interface to corporate supplier processes
- Maintaining and reviewing a Supplier and Contracts Database (SCD), with review and Risk Analysis of all suppliers and contracts on a regular basis
- Ensuring that underpinning contracts, agreements or SLAs are aligned with those of the business

- Ensuring that all supporting services are scoped and documented, and that interfaces and dependencies between suppliers, supporting services and supplier processes are documented
- Reviewing lead suppliers' processes to ensure that any sub-contracted suppliers are meeting their contractual obligations, with documented roles and responsibilities
- Performing contract or SLA reviews at least annually, and ensuring that all contracts are consistent with organizational requirements and standard terms and conditions wherever possible
- Maintaining a process for dealing with contractual disputes and contract termination, ensuring that any disputes are dealt with in an efficient and effective manner
- Monitoring, reporting and regularly reviewing supplier performance against targets, identifying improvement actions as appropriate and ensuring these actions are implemented
- Coordinating and supporting all individual IT supplier and contract managers, ensuring that each supplier/contract has a nominated owner within the service provider organization.

3.6 SERVICE DESIGN MODELS

The model selected for the design of IT services will depend mainly on the model selected for the delivery of IT services. Before adopting a design model for a major new service, the current capability of the service provider should be reviewed. This review/assessment provides a structured mechanism for determining an organization's capabilities and state of readiness for delivering new or revised services in support of defined business drivers and requirements. The information obtained from such an assessment can be used in determining the delivery strategy for a particular new IT service or IT system. The delivery strategy is the approach taken to move an organization from a known state, based on the readiness assessment, to a desired state, determined by the business drivers and needs. Although several options are available, not every option needs be considered. However, keeping all the options available is key to designing innovative solutions (Table 3.1).

Table 3.1 Main service delivery strategies

Delivery strategy	Description
Insourcing	This approach relies on utilizing internal organizational resources in the design, development, transition and operation of new or changed services
Outsourcing	This approach utilizes the resources of an external organization or organizations in a formal arrangement to provide a well-defined portion of a service's design, development and operation
Co-sourcing	Often the approach utilizes a combination of insourcing and outsourcing, with a number of outsourcing organizations working together to co-source key elements within the lifecycle
Partnership or multi-sourcing	This approach involves formal strategic partnership arrangements between two or more organizations to work together to design, develop, transition and operate IT service(s)
Business Process Outsourcing (BPO)	This is the increasing trend of relocating entire business functions using formal arrangements between organizations, where one organization provides and manages the other organization's entire business process(es) or function(s)

Application Service Provision	This approach involves formal arrangements with an Application Service Provider (ASP) organization that will provide shared computer-based services to customer organizations over a network, sometimes referred to as on-demand.
Knowledge Process Outsourcing (KPO)	KPO is a step ahead of BPO in one respect. KPO organizations provide domain-based processes and business expertise, requiring specialized skills.

Table 3.1 highlights a key point: delivery strategies vary widely and range from a relatively straightforward situation, solely managed within the boundaries of a company, all the way to a full KPO situation. This broad range of alternatives provides significant flexibility, but often with added complexity, and in some cases additional risk. All of the above arrangements can be provided in both an off-shore or on-shore situation. The delivery strategies listed in Table 3.1 are relevant to both the design and transition stages of the Service Lifecycle as well as the operation stage. Extreme care must be taken when selecting different strategies for different stages of the lifecycle to ensure that all the organizations involved clearly understand their individual roles and responsibilities.

3.6.1 Design and development approaches

It is important to understand the current generic lifecycle types, methods and approaches to IT service development, in order to decide on standards for the Service Design stage of the lifecycle. To achieve this, a good understanding is needed of the various Service Development Lifecycle (SDLC) approaches.

Rapid Application Development

The main feature of Rapid Application Development (RAD) is the introduction of increments and iterations in the development process for the management of the risks associated with uncertainty and changing requirements. Traditional approaches have assumed that a complete set of requirements could be defined early in the lifecycle and that development costs could be controlled by managing change. However, discouraging change can mean being unresponsive to business conditions. RAD accepts that change is inevitable, and attempts to minimize the costs while retaining quality.

The use of increments implies that a service is developed piece by piece, where every piece could support one of the business functions that the entire service needs. Incremental delivery could result in shorter time to market for specific business functions. The development of every increment requires traversal of all lifecycle stages. To make good use of an incremental approach, the design process needs to be based on a separation of concerns, by grouping functions within increments in such a way that their interdependence is minimized. In general terms, accelerated application development methods adopt a three-phase lifecycle model: accelerated analysis and design, time-boxed development, and production and implementation.

Off-the-shelf solutions

Many organizations now choose to fulfil their IT service requirements through the purchasing and implementing of commercial off-the-shelf (COTS) software package solutions. A framework for selecting, customizing and implementing these off-the-shelf packaged solutions needs to be comprehensive and should include all aspects of the solution and its subsequent transition, operation and improvement.

3.7 SERVICE DESIGN PROCESS ELEMENTS

This section describes and explains the fundamentals of the key supporting Service Design processes. These processes are principally responsible for providing key information to the design of new or changed service solutions, taking into consideration the five aspects of design.

In order to develop effective and efficient service solutions that meet and continue to meet the requirements of the business and the needs of IT, it is essential that all the inputs and needs of all other areas and processes are considered within each of the Service Design activities, as illustrated in Figure 3.11. This will ensure that all service solutions are consistent and compatible with existing solutions and will meet the expectations of the customers and users. This will most effectively be achieved by consolidating these facets of the key processes into all of these Service Design activities, so that all inputs are automatically referenced every time a new or changed service solution is produced.

3.7.1 Service Catalogue Management

The Service Catalogue provides a central source of information on the IT services delivered by the service provider organization. This ensures that all areas of the business can view an accurate, consistent picture of the IT services, their details and their status. It contains a customer-facing view of the IT services in use, how they are intended to be used, the business processes they enable, and the levels and quality of service the customer can expect for each service.

Figure 3.11 Service Design – the big picture

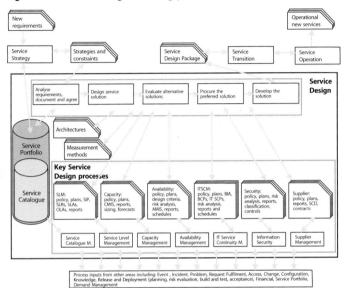

The objective of Service Catalogue Management (SCM) is to manage
the information contained within the Service Catalogue, and to ensure that
it is accurate and reflects the current details, status, interfaces and
dependencies of all services that are being run, or being prepared to
run, in the live environment.

The scope of the SCM process is to provide and maintain accurate information on all services that are being transitioned or have been transitioned to the live environment.

The Service Catalogue has two aspects, which are summarized below and in Figure 3.12:

- **Business Service Catalogue** – this contains details of all the IT services delivered to the customer, together with relationships to the business units and the business process
- **Technical Service Catalogue** – this contains details of all the IT services delivered to the customer, together with relationships to the supporting services, IT systems and components.

Figure 3.12 The Business Service Catalogue and the Technical Service Catalogue

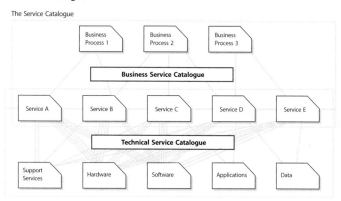

Some organizations maintain either a Business Service Catalogue or a Technical Service Catalogue. The preferred approach of the more mature organizations is to maintain both aspects within a single Service Catalogue, which is part of a Service Portfolio. The Business Service Catalogue facilitates the development of a much more proactive set of Business Service Management (BSM) activities, whereas the Technical Service Catalogue allows the impact of IT systems and components on services to be more clearly understood.

Service Catalogue Management process characteristics

The key activities within SCM are:

- Agreeing and documenting a service definition with all relevant parties
- Interfacing with Service Portfolio Management (SPM) to agree the contents of the Service Portfolio
- Maintaining a Service Catalogue and its contents, in line with the Service Portfolio
- Interfacing with the business on the dependencies of business units and their business processes
- Interfacing with support teams and suppliers on dependencies between IT services and systems
- Interfacing with Business Relationship Management (BRM) and SLM to ensure that information is aligned to the business.

The key information within the SCM process is that contained within the Service Catalogue. The main input for this information comes from the Service Portfolio and the business via either the BRM or SLM processes.

A number of sources of information are relevant to the SCM process, including:

- Business information from the organization's business and IT strategy, plans and financial plans
- Business Impact Analysis (BIA), on the service impacts, priorities and risks
- Business requirements on new or changed business requirements
- The Service Portfolio
- The Configuration Management System (CMS)

- Feedback from all other processes and the SKMS.

The principal triggers for the SCM process are changes in the business requirements and services. The process outputs of SCM are:

- The documentation and agreement of a 'definition of the service'
- Updates to the Service Portfolio, and service status
- The Service Catalogue, which should contain the details and the current status of every live service provided by the service provider.

The two main key performance indicators (KPIs) associated with the Service Catalogue and its management are:

- The number of services recorded and managed within the Service Catalogue as a percentage of those being delivered and transitioned in the live environment
- The number of variances detected between the information contained within the Service Catalogue and the 'real-world' situation.

The main Critical Success Factors (CSFs) for the SCM process are:

- An accurate Service Catalogue
- Business users' awareness of the services being provided
- IT staff awareness of the technology supporting the services.

The risks associated with the provision of an accurate Service Catalogue are:

- Inaccuracy of the data in the catalogue, and the data not being under rigorous Change Management
- Inaccurate information received from the business, IT and the Service Portfolio
- The tools and resources required to maintain the information
- Poor access to accurate Change Management, CMS and SKMS information
- Circumvention of the use of the Service Portfolio and Service Catalogue in operational processes
- The information is either too detailed to maintain accurately or at too high a level.

3.7.2 Service Level Management

SLM negotiates, agrees and documents appropriate IT service targets with representatives of the business, and then monitors and produces reports on the service provider's ability to deliver the agreed level of service. The purpose of the SLM process is to ensure that all operational services and their performance are measured in a consistent, professional manner throughout the IT organization, and that the services and the reports produced meet the needs of the business and customers.

The objectives of SLM are to:

- Document, agree, monitor, measure, report and review the level of service
- Provide and improve the relationship and communication with the business
- Ensure that specific and measurable targets are developed for all IT services
- Monitor and improve customer satisfaction with the quality of service
- Ensure everyone has the same expectation of the level of service
- Ensure proactive measures to improve the levels of service are implemented.

An SLA is a written agreement between an IT service provider and the IT customer(s), defining the key service targets and responsibilities of both parties. The emphasis must be on agreement, and SLAs should not be used as a way of holding one side or the other to ransom. A true partnership should be developed between the IT service provider and the customer, so that a mutually beneficial agreement is reached. SLM is also responsible for ensuring that all targets and measures agreed in SLAs with the business are supported by appropriate underpinning OLAs or contracts, with internal support units and external partners and suppliers (Figure 3.13).

Figure 3.13 Service Level Management

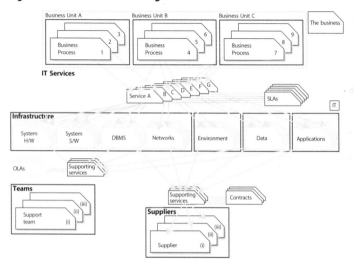

The key activities within the SLM process should include:

- Determining, negotiating, documenting and agreeing requirements for new or changed services in SLRs
- Monitoring and measuring service achievements of all operational services against targets within SLAs
- Collating, measuring and improving customer satisfaction
- Producing service reports
- Conducting service reviews and instigating improvements in an overall Service Improvement Plan (SIP)
- Reviewing and revising SLAs, service scope OLAs, contracts, and any other underpinning agreements
- Developing and documenting contacts and relationships with the business, customers and stakeholders

- Developing, maintaining and operating procedures for managing all complaints and compliments
- Providing appropriate information to aid management and demonstrate service achievement
- Making available and maintaining up-to-date SLM document templates and standards.

The interfaces between the main SLM activities are summarized below and in Figure 3.14.

Figure 3.14 The Service Level Management process

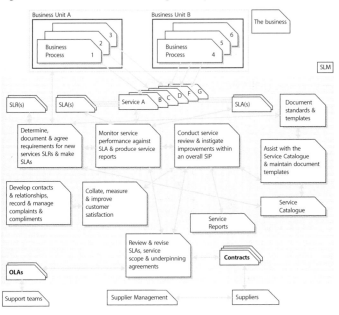

Designing SLA frameworks

Using the Service Catalogue, SLM must design appropriate SLA structures to ensure that services and customers are covered in a manner best suited to the organization's needs. The main options are:

■ **Service-based SLAs** – an SLA for all the customers of a service
■ **Customer-based SLAs** – an SLA with a customer group, covering all services
■ **Multi-level SLAs: SLAs** – based on corporate, customer and service SLAs (Figure 3.15).

Figure 3.15 Multi-level SLAs

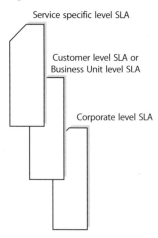

Service specific level SLA

Customer level SLA or
Business Unit level SLA

Corporate level SLA

Many organizations have found it valuable to produce standards and a set of templates that can be used as a starting point for all SLAs, SLRs and OLAs. The wording of SLAs should be clear and concise. Where the IT services are provided to another organization by an external service provider, sometimes the service targets are contained within a contract or within an attached SLA or schedule.

SLM process characteristics

There are many triggers that instigate SLM activity. These include:

- Changes in the Service Portfolio, such as new or changed business requirements or services
- New or changed agreements, SLRs, SLAs, OLAs or contracts
- Service review meetings and actions
- Periodic activities – reporting and customer satisfaction surveys, compliments and complaints
- Changes in strategy or policy.

A number of sources of information are relevant to the SLM process. These should include:

- Business information – from the organization's business strategy, plans and financial plans
- BIA – on service impacts, priorities, risks and numbers of users
- Business requirements – details of any agreed, new or changed business requirements
- The Service Portfolio and strategies, policies and constraints from Service Strategy
- Change information – the Change Schedule from Change Management
- CMS – information on the relationships between business services and supporting systems
- Customer and user feedback, complaints and compliments
- Other inputs – including advice, information and input from any of the other processes.

The outputs of SLM should include:

- Service reports – providing details of the service levels achieved in relation to SLA targets

- SIP – an overall programme or plan of improvements
- The Service Quality Plan – documenting and planning overall improvements of service quality
- Document templates – standard templates, format and content for SLAs, SLRs and OLAs
- SLAs, SLRs and OLAs providing targets for services and support teams
- Reports on OLAs and underpinning contracts
- Service review, SLA review and service scope review meeting minutes and actions
- Revised contracts – resulting from changes to SLAs or new SLRs.

Metrics should be developed from the service, customer and business perspective, and should cover both objective and subjective measurements, such as:

- **Objective** – the percentage of service targets met, the number and severity of breaches, the number of up-to-date SLAs and the number of timely reports and reviews
- **Subjective** – improvements in customer satisfaction and perception.

The SLM process often generates a good starting point for a SIP – and the service review process may drive this; however, all processes and all areas of the service provider organization should be involved in the SIP. SLM provides key information on all operational services, their expected targets and the service achievements and breaches for all operational services. It provides the information and trends on customer satisfaction, including complaints and compliments, the quality of IT service provided to the customer and the customer's expectation and perception of that quality of service.

The main CSFs for the SLM process are:

- Managing the overall quality of IT services required
- Delivering the service as previously agreed at affordable costs
- Managing the interface with the business and users.

The risks associated with SLM are:

- Lack of accurate input, involvement and commitment from the business
- Lack of tools and resources required to agree, report and review SLAs and service levels
- The process being a bureaucratic, administrative process rather than an active and proactive one
- Access to and support of appropriate and up-to-date CMS and SKMS
- Bypassing the use of the SLM processes
- Business and customer measurements being too difficult to measure and improve
- Inappropriate business and customer contacts and relationships
- High customer expectations and low perception
- Poor and inappropriate communication with the business and customers.

3.7.3   Capacity Management

Capacity Management is a process that extends across the Service Lifecycle. A key success factor in managing capacity is ensuring it is considered during the design stage. Capacity Management is supported initially in Service Strategy where the decisions and analysis of business requirements and customer outcomes influence the development of patterns of business activity, levels of service and service level packages. This provides the predictive and ongoing capacity indicators that are needed to align capacity to demand. The purpose of Capacity Management is to provide a point of focus and management for all capacity- and performance-related issues, with regard to both services and resources.

The objectives of Capacity Management are to:

- Produce and maintain an appropriate and up-to-date Capacity Plan
- Provide advice and guidance IT on all capacity- and performance-related issues
- Ensure that service performance achievements meet or exceed targets
- Assist with the diagnosis and resolution of performance issues

- Assess the impact of changes on the Capacity Plan and service performance
- Ensure proactive measures to improve the performance are implemented.

The Capacity Management process should include:

- Monitoring patterns of business activity and service level plans through performance, utilization and throughput of IT services and components, and the production of reports
- Undertaking tuning activities to make the most efficient use of existing IT resources
- Understanding the agreed current and future demands on IT resources, and producing forecasts
- Influencing Demand Management, perhaps in conjunction with Financial Management
- Producing a Capacity Plan that enables the service provider to continue to provide services of the quality defined in SLAs and SLRs
- Assistance with the identification and resolution of any service or component performance issues
- The proactive improvement of service or component performance wherever it is cost-justifiable.

Capacity Management provides the necessary information on current and planned resource utilization of individual components to enable organizations to decide, with confidence, which components and services to upgrade, within what timeframe and at what cost. Capacity Management is one of the forward-looking processes that, when properly carried out, can forecast the impact of business events and impacts often before they happen. Good Capacity Management ensures that there are no surprises with regard to service and component design and performance. In conjunction with the business and their plans, Capacity Management provides a Capacity Plan that outlines the IT resources and funding needed to support the business plan and services, together with a justification of the costs. Capacity Management ensures that the capacity and performance of the IT services and systems match the evolving agreed demands of the business in the most cost-effective and timely manner. Capacity Management is essentially a balancing act:

- Balancing costs against resources needed
- Balancing supply against demand.

Capacity Management processes and planning must be involved in all stages of the Service Lifecycle from Strategy and Design, through Transition and Operation to Improvement. From a strategic perspective, the Service Portfolio contains the IT resources and capabilities. Service Oriented Architecture, virtualization and the use of value networks in IT service provision are important factors in the management of capacity. Appropriate capacity and performance should be designed into services and components from the initial design stages. This will ensure not only that the performance of any new or changed service meets its expected targets, but also that all existing services continue to meet all of their targets. This is the basis of stable service provision. The overall Capacity Management process is continually trying cost-effectively to match IT resources and capacity to the ever-changing needs and requirements of the business. Capacity Management is an extremely technical, complex and demanding process, and in order to achieve results, it requires three supporting sub-processes:

- Business Capacity Management – this focuses on the current and future business requirements
- Service Capacity Management – this focuses on the delivery of the existing services that support the business
- Component Capacity Management – this focuses on the IT infrastructure that underpins service provision.

The tools used by Capacity Management should conform to the organization's management architecture and integrate with other tools used for the management of IT systems and automation of IT processes. These tools are used to support both the reactive and proactive activities of Capacity Management (see Figure 3.16).

Business Capacity Management

This sub-process translates business needs and plans into requirements for service and IT infrastructure, ensuring that the future business requirements for IT services are quantified, designed, planned and implemented in a timely fashion. The main objective of the Business Capacity Management sub-process is to ensure that the future business requirements (customer outcomes) for IT services are considered and understood, and that sufficient IT capacity to support any new or changed services is planned and implemented within an appropriate timescale. These new requirements may come from many different sources and for many different reasons, but the principal sources of supply should be the Pattern of Business Activity (PBA) from Demand Management and the Service Level Packages (SLPs) produced for the Service Portfolio.

Service Capacity Management

The focus of this sub-process is the management, control and prediction of the end-to-end performance and capacity of the live, operational IT service usage and workloads. The main objective of the Service Capacity Management sub-process is to identify and understand the IT services, their use of resource, working patterns, peaks and troughs, and to ensure that the services meet their SLA targets. In this sub-process, the focus is on managing service performance, as determined by the targets contained in the agreed SLAs or SLRs. The monitoring of services provides data that can identify trends from which normal service levels can be established. By regular monitoring, and comparison with these levels, exception conditions can be defined, identified and reported on.

Component Capacity Management

The focus in this sub-process is the management, control and prediction of the performance, utilization and capacity of individual IT technology components. The main objective of Component Capacity Management is to identify and understand the performance, capacity and utilization of each of the individual components within the technology used to support the IT services, including the infrastructure, environment, data and applications. This ensures the optimum use of the current hardware and software resources in order to achieve and maintain the agreed service levels. All hardware components and many software components in the IT infrastructure have a finite capacity that, when approached or exceeded, has the potential to cause performance problems.

A number of the activities need to be carried out iteratively and form a natural cycle, as illustrated in Figure 3.16. The proactive activities of Capacity Management should include:

- Pre-empting performance issues by taking the necessary actions before they occur
- Measuring using trends and thresholds for planning future upgrades and enhancements
- Modelling and trending the predicted changes in IT services identifying the changes needed
- Ensuring that upgrades are planned and implemented before SLAs and service targets are breached
- Actively seeking to improve service performance wherever it is cost-justifiable
- Tuning and optimizing the performance of services and components.

The reactive activities of Capacity Management should include:

- Monitoring, measuring, reporting and reviewing current service and component performance
- Responding to all capacity-related 'threshold' events and instigating corrective action

■ Reacting to and assisting with specific performance issues.

Figure 3.16 Iterative ongoing activities of Capacity Management

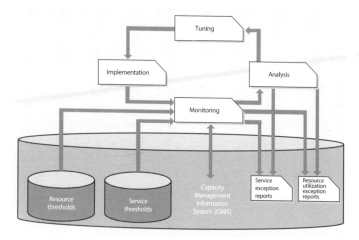

These activities provide the basic historical information and triggers that are necessary for all of the other activities and processes within Capacity Management. Monitors should be established on all the components and for each of the services. The data should be analysed using, wherever possible, expert systems to compare usage levels against thresholds. The results of the analysis should be included in reports, and recommendations made as appropriate. Some form of control mechanism may then be put in place to act on the recommendations. This may take the form of balancing services, balancing workloads, changing concurrency levels and adding or removing resources. All of the information accumulated during these activities should be stored in the Capacity Management Information System (CMIS), and the cycle then begins again.

Capacity Management process characteristics

There are many triggers that will initiate Capacity Management activities. These include:

- Service breaches, capacity or performance events and alerts, including threshold events
- Exception reports
- Revision of current capacity and performance and the review of forecasts, reports and plans
- New and changed services requiring additional capacity
- Periodic trending and modelling
- Review and revision of business and IT plans and strategies, and designs and strategies
- Review and revision of SLAs, OLAs, contracts or any other agreements.

A number of sources of input are relevant to the Capacity Management process:

- Business information – including strategies, plans and financial plans
- Service and IT information – from Service Strategy, the IT strategy and plans, and current budgets
- Component performance and capacity information – on all services and technologies
- Service performance issues – relating to poor performance
- Service information – from the SLM process, with details of the services from SLAs and SLRs
- Financial information – the cost of service provision, the cost of resources and upgrades
- Change information – the Change Schedule from Change Management
- Performance information – the CMIS on the current performance of services and components
- CMS – information and relationships between the business, the services, the supporting technology
- Workload information – schedules of all the work that needs to be run and the interdependencies.

The outputs of Capacity Management are used within all other parts of the process, and include:

- The CMIS – holds the information needed by all sub-processes within Capacity Management
- The Capacity Plan – used by all areas of the business and IT management
- Service performance information and reports – used by many other processes
- Workload analysis and reports – to assess and implement changes in work schedules
- Capacity and performance reports – used by all areas to analyse and resolve performance issues
- Forecasts and predictive reports – used by all areas to analyse, predict and forecast scenarios
- Thresholds, alerts and events.

Some of the main CSFs, KPIs and metrics that can be used to judge the efficiency and effectiveness of the Capacity Management activities are:

- Accurate business forecasts:
  - Percentage accuracy and timeliness of forecasts of business trends
  - Timely incorporation of business plans into the Capacity Plan
  - Reduction in the number of variances from the business plans and Capacity Plans
- Knowledge of current and future technologies:
  - Increased ability to monitor performance and throughput of all services and components
  - Timely justification and implementation of new technology in line with business needs
  - Reduction in the use of old technology, causing breached SLAs due to performance

- Ability to demonstrate cost-effectiveness:
  - Reduction in last-minute buying to address urgent performance issues
  - Reduction in the over-capacity of IT
  - Accurate forecasts of planned expenditure
  - Reduction in the business disruption caused by a lack of adequate IT capacity
- Ability to plan and implement the appropriate IT capacity to match business needs:
  - Percentage reduction in the number of Incidents due to poor performance
  - Percentage reduction in lost business due to inadequate capacity
  - All new services implemented match Service Level Requirements (SLRs)
  - Reduction in the number of SLA breaches due to poor service or component performance.

The CMIS is the cornerstone of a successful Capacity Management process. Information contained within the CMIS is stored and analysed by all the sub-processes of Capacity Management because it is a repository of many different types of data, including business, service and component utilization and financial data, from all areas of technology. However, the CMIS is unlikely to be a single database, and probably exists in several physical locations. Data from all areas of technology, and all components that make up the IT services, can then be combined for analysis and provision of technical and management reporting.

Some of the major risks associated with Capacity Management are:

- Lack of commitment from the business to the Capacity Management process
- Lack of appropriate information from the business on plans and strategies
- Lack of senior management commitment or lack of resources or budget
- SCM and Component Capacity Management performed in isolation because BCM is difficult
- The processes become too bureaucratic or manually intensive

- The processes focus too much on technology and not on services and the business
- The reports and information provided are too bulky or too technical.

3.7.4 Availability Management

The goal of the AM process is to ensure that the level of service availability delivered in all services is matched to, or exceeds, the current and future agreed needs of the business, and in a cost-effective manner. The purpose of AM is to provide a point of focus and management for all availability-related issues, with regard to both services and resources, ensuring that availability targets in all areas are measured and achieved.

The objectives of AM are to:

- Produce and maintain an appropriate and up-to-date Availability Plan that reflects the current and future needs of the business
- Provide advice and guidance to all areas of the business and IT on all availability-related issues
- Ensure that service availability achievements meet or exceed all their agreed targets
- Assist with the diagnosis and resolution of availability-related Incidents and Problems
- Assess the impact of all changes on the Availability Plan and the performance of all services
- Ensure proactive improvements to service availability are implemented wherever possible.

AM should ensure the agreed level of availability is provided. The measurement and monitoring of IT availability is a key activity to ensure availability levels are being met consistently. AM should look to continually optimize and proactively improve the availability of the IT infrastructure, the services and the supporting organization, in order to provide cost-effective availability improvements that can deliver business and customer benefits.

The scope of the AM process covers the design, implementation, measurement, management and improvement of IT service and component availability. AM needs to understand the service and component availability requirements from the business perspective. Understanding this will enable AM to ensure that all the services and components are designed and delivered to meet their targets in terms of agreed business needs. The AM process should be applied to all new and operational services, support services and technology, particularly those covered by SLAs, SLRs, OLAs and contracts. It can also be applied to those IT services deemed to be business critical, regardless of whether formal SLAs exist.

The AM process should include:

- Monitoring of all aspects of availability, reliability and maintainability of services and components
- Maintenance of a set of methods, techniques and calculations for all availability measurements
- Assistance with risk assessment and management activities
- Collection of measurements, analysis and production of regular and ad hoc availability reports
- Understanding the agreed current and future demands of the business for IT services availability
- Influencing the design of services and components to align with business needs
- Producing an Availability Plan that enables the continued provision and improvement of services
- Maintaining a schedule of tests for all resilient and fail-over components and mechanisms
- Assisting with the identification and resolution of any unavailability Incidents and Problems
- Proactive improvement of service or component availability wherever it is cost-justifiable.

The AM process ensures that the availability of systems and services matches the evolving agreed needs of the business. The availability and reliability of IT services can directly influence customer satisfaction and the reputation of the business. In today's competitive marketplace, customer satisfaction with service(s) provided is paramount. Customer loyalty can no longer be relied on, and dissatisfaction with the availability and reliability of IT service can be a key factor in customer retention. The AM process and planning, just like Capacity Management, must be involved in all stages of the Service Lifecycle, from Strategy and Design, through Transition and Operation to Improvement. The appropriate availability and resilience should be designed into services and components from the initial design stages. In order to achieve this, AM should perform both reactive and proactive activities (Figure 3.17).

Figure 3.17 The Availability Management process

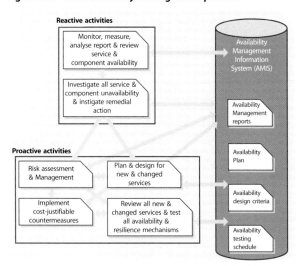

The scope of AM covers the design, implementation, measurement and management of IT service and infrastructure availability. This is summarized below and in Figure 3.18.

The AM process has two key elements:

- **Reactive activities** – the reactive aspect of AM involves monitoring, measuring, analysis and management of events, Incidents and Problems involving unavailability
- **Proactive activities** – the proactive activities of AM include the proactive planning, design, recommendation, criteria and improvement of availability.

AM is completed at two interconnected levels:

- **Service availability** – this involves all aspects of service availability and unavailability and the impact of component availability, or the potential impact of component unavailability, on service availability
- **Component availability** – this involves all aspects of component availability and unavailability.

AM relies on the monitoring, measurement, analysis and reporting of the following aspects:

- **Availability** – the ability of a service, component or Configuration Item to perform its agreed function
- **Reliability** – a measure of the ability of a service or a component to perform its agreed function
- **Maintainability** – the time taken to restore a service or component to normal working
- **Serviceability** – the ability of a third-party supplier to meet the terms of its contract.

Figure 3.18 Availability terms and measurements

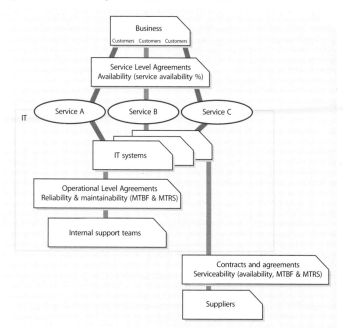

Although the principal service target contained within SLAs for the customers and the business is availability, as illustrated in Figure 3.18, some customers also require reliability and maintainability targets to be included. When these targets are included in SLAs, they should relate to service reliability and maintainability targets; reliability and maintainability targets contained in OLAs and contracts relate to component and supporting service targets and can often include availability targets relating to the relevant components or supporting services.

The term Vital Business Function (VBF) is used to reflect the business critical elements of the business process supported by an IT service. Generally, the more vital the business function, the greater the level of resilience and availability that must be incorporated into the design required in the supporting IT services. For all services, whether VBFs or not, the availability requirements should be determined by the business and not by IT, and may need special designs:

- **High availability** – an IT service that minimizes or masks the effects of IT component failure
- **Fault tolerance** – ability of an IT service to continue operating after component failure
- **Continuous operation** – an approach or design to eliminate planned downtime of an IT service
- **Continuous availability** – an approach or design to achieve 100% availability.

AM commences as soon as the availability requirements for an IT service are clear enough to be articulated. It is an ongoing process, finishing only when the IT service is decommissioned or retired. The key activities of the AM process are:

- Determining the availability requirements from the business for a new or enhanced IT
- Determining the VBFs, in conjunction with the business and ITSCM
- Determining the impact arising from IT service and component failure
- Defining the targets for availability, reliability and maintainability for the IT technology
- Establishing measures and reporting of availability, reliability and maintainability
- Monitoring and trend analysis of the availability, reliability and maintainability of IT components
- Reviewing IT service and component availability and identifying unacceptable levels
- Investigating the underlying reasons for unacceptable availability

■ Producing and maintaining an Availability Plan that plans and improves IT availability.

The AM process depends heavily on the measurement of service and component achievements with regard to availability.

'What to measure and how to report it' inevitably depends on which activity is being supported, who the recipients are and how the information is to be utilized. It is important to recognize the differing perspectives of availability to ensure measurement and reporting satisfies the needs from the business perspective, the customer perspective and the IT service provider perspective.

Reactive activities of AM

■ **Monitor, measure, analyse and report service and component availability** – a key output from the AM process is the measurement and reporting of IT availability. Availability measures should be incorporated into SLAs, OLAs and any underpinning contracts. These should be reviewed regularly at Service Level review meetings. The business may have, for many years, accepted that the IT availability it experiences is represented in terms of component availability rather than overall service or business availability. However, this is no longer being viewed as acceptable and the business is keen to better represent availability in measure(s) that demonstrate the positive and negative consequences of IT availability on the business and the users

■ **Unavailability analysis** – all events and Incidents causing unavailability of services and components should be investigated, with remedial actions being implemented within either the Availability Plan or the overall SIP. Trends should be produced from this analysis to direct and focus activities such as Service Failure Analysis (SFA) to those areas causing the most impact or disruption to the business and the users. The overall costs of an IT service are influenced by the levels of availability required. Availability certainly does not come for free. However, it is important to reflect that the unavailability of IT also has a cost, therefore unavailability also is not free. For optimum performance, the costs of the availability solution must be balanced against the costs of unavailability

■ **The Expanded Incident Lifecycle** – a guiding principle of AM is to recognize that it is still possible to gain customer satisfaction when things go wrong. An aim of AM should be to ensure that the duration of and impact from Incidents affecting IT services are minimized to enable business operations to resume as quickly as is possible. The analysis of the Expanded Incident Lifecycle allows the total IT service downtime for any given Incident to be broken down and mapped against the major stages through which all Incidents progress.
AM should work closely with Incident Management and Problem Management in the analysis of all Incidents causing unavailability in order to reduce each stage involved within the lifecycle (Figure 3.19)

Figure 3.19 The Expanded Incident Lifecycle

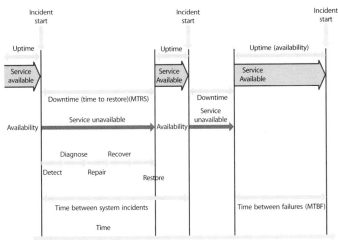

- **Service Failure Analysis (SFA)** – This technique provides a structured approach to identify the underlying causes of service interruptions to the user. SFA utilizes a range of data sources to assess where and why shortfalls in availability are occurring. SFA enables a holistic view to be taken – to drive not just technology improvements but also improvements to the IT support organization, processes, procedures and tools. The detailed analysis of service interruptions can identify opportunities to enhance levels of availability.

Proactive activities of AM

- **Identifying VBFs** – the term Vital Business Function is used to reflect the business critical elements of the business process supported by an IT service. The service may also support less critical business functions and processes, and it is important that the VBFs are recognized and documented to provide the appropriate business alignment and focus

- **Designing for availability** – the level of availability required by the business influences the overall cost of the IT service provided. In general, the higher the level of availability required by the business, the higher the cost. These costs are not just the procurement of the base IT technology and services required to underpin the IT infrastructure. Additional costs are incurred in providing the appropriate Service Management processes, systems management tools and high-availability solutions required to meet the more stringent availability requirements. The greatest level of availability should be included in the design of those services supporting the most critical VBFs. It is also important to recognize that there is a cost to the business for loss of service (unavailability; see Figure 3.20) and that this cost must be factored into the design to determine the optimal level of risk, cost and benefit.

Figure 3.20 Relationship between levels of availability and overall costs

AM process characteristics

Many events may trigger AM activity. These include:

- New or changed business needs or new or changed services
- New or changed targets within agreements, such as SLRs, SLAs, OLAs or contracts
- Service or component breaches, availability events and alerts, including threshold events
- Periodic activities such as reviewing, revising or reporting
- Review of AM forecasts, reports and plans

- Review and revision of business and IT plans and strategies
- Review and revision of designs and strategies
- Recognition or notification of a change of risk or impact of a business process or VBF
- Request from SLM for assistance with availability targets and explanation of achievements.

A number of sources of input are relevant to the AM process:

- **Business information** – from the organization's business strategy, plans and financial plans
- **Business impact information** – from Business Impact Analyses and assessment of VBFs underpinned by IT services
- **Previous Risk Analysis** and Assessment reports and a Risk Register
- **Service information** – from the Service Portfolio and the Service Catalogue
- **Service information** – SLAs, SLRs, and OLAs and service level targets
- **Financial information** – the cost of service provision and the cost of resources and components
- **Change and release information** – with a Change Schedule, and the Release Schedule
- **Configuration Management** – information on the relationships between the business and services
- **Component information** – on the availability, reliability and maintainability requirements
- **Technology information** – from the CMS on the topology and the relationships
- **Past performance** – from previous measurements on availability achievements and reports
- **Unavailability and failure information** – from Incidents and Problems and service breaches.

The outputs produced by AM should include:

- The AMIS
- The Availability Plan for the proactive improvement of IT services and technology
- Availability and recovery design criteria and proposed service targets for new or changed services
- Service availability, reliability and maintainability reports of achievements against targets
- Component availability, reliability and maintainability reports of achievements against targets
- Revised risk analysis reviews and reports and an updated Risk Register
- Monitoring, management and reporting requirements for IT services and components
- An AM test schedule for testing all availability and recovery mechanisms
- The planned and preventive maintenance schedules
- The Projected Service Outage (PSO) in conjunction with Change and Release Management
- Details of the proactive availability techniques and measures that will be deployed
- Improvement actions for inclusion within the SIP.

Many CSFs and KPIs can be used to measure the effectiveness and efficiency of AM, including:

- Management of availability and reliability of IT service:
  - Effective review and follow-up of all SLA, OLA and underpinning contract breaches
  - Percentage reduction in the number and impact of service breaks
  - Improvement in the reliability of services, MTBF (Mean Time Between Failures)
  - Reduction in the maintainability, MTRS (Mean Time to Restore Service)

- ■ Satisfying business needs for access to IT services:
  - − Percentage reduction in the unavailability of services and components
  - − Percentage reduction of the cost of business overtime due to unavailable IT
  - − Percentage improvement in business and users satisfied with service
- ■ Availability of IT infrastructure achieved at optimum costs:
  - − Percentage reduction in the cost of unavailability
  - − Timely completion of regular Risk Analysis and system review
  - − Timely completion of regular Component Failure Impact Analysis (CFIA) and cost–benefit analysis
  - − Percentage reduction in failures of third-party performance on MTRS/MTBF
  - − Reduced time taken to complete an Availability Plan.

The AMIS should contain all of the measurements and information required to complete the AM process and to present appropriate information to the business on the level of IT service provided. This information – covering services, components and supporting services – provides the basis for regular, ad hoc and exception availability reporting and the identification of trends within the data for the instigation of improvement activities. These activities and the information contained within the AMIS provide the basis for developing the content of the Availability Plan.

AM faces many challenges, but probably the main challenge is to meet the expectations of the customers, the business and senior management. This can be achieved only when the appropriate level of investment and design has been applied to the service, which should be done only where the business impact justifies that level of investment. Another challenge facing AM is the integration of all of the availability data into an integrated set of information (AMIS) that can be analysed in a consistent manner to provide details on the availability of all services and components. This is particularly challenging when the information from the different technologies is often provided by different tools in differing formats. Yet another challenge facing AM is convincing the business and senior management of the investment needed in proactive availability measures.

Some of the major risks associated with AM are:

- Lack of commitment from the business to the AM process
- Lack of commitment from the business and lack of appropriate information on future plans and strategies
- Lack of senior management commitment or lack of resources and/or budget
- The reporting processes become very labour-intensive
- The processes focus too much on the technology and not enough on the business and service needs
- The AMIS is maintained in isolation and is not shared or consistent with other process areas.

3.7.5   IT Service Continuity Management

The goal of ITSCM is to support the overall BCM process by ensuring that the required IT technical and service facilities can be resumed within required, and agreed, business timescales. As technology is a core component of most business processes, continued or high availability of IT is critical to the survival of the business as a whole. This is achieved by introducing risk reduction measures and recovery options. Ongoing maintenance of the recovery capability is essential if it is to remain effective. The purpose of ITSCM is to maintain the necessary ongoing recovery capability within the IT services and their supporting components.

The objectives of ITSCM are to:

- Maintain a set of IT Service Continuity Plans (IT SCPs) and IT recovery plans that support the business plans
- Complete BIA exercises to ensure plans are in line with business needs
- Conduct regular Risk Analysis and Management exercises, to manage service risks

- Provide advice and guidance to all other areas of the business and IT on all continuity issues
- Ensure that continuity and recovery mechanisms are put in place to meet business targets
- Assess the impact of all changes on the IT SCPs and IT recovery plans
- Ensure that proactive measures to improve service availability are implemented wherever possible
- Negotiate and agree contracts with suppliers for the provision of recovery capability.

ITSCM focuses on those events that are significant enough to be considered as a disaster by the business. The scope of ITSCM within an organization is determined by the organizational structure, culture and strategic direction (both business and technology) in terms of the services provided and how these develop and change over time.

The ITSCM process should be driven by business risk as identified by Business Continuity Planning, and ensures that the recovery arrangements for IT services are aligned to identified business impacts, risks and needs. A lifecycle approach should be adopted to the setting up and operation of an ITSCM process. Figure 3.21 shows the lifecycle of ITSCM, from initiation through to continual assurance that the protection provided is current and reflects all changes to services and service levels. ITSCM is a cyclic process throughout the lifecycle to ensure once service continuity and recovery plans have been developed they are kept aligned with BCPs and business priorities.

Figure 3.21 Lifecycle of IT Service Continuity Management

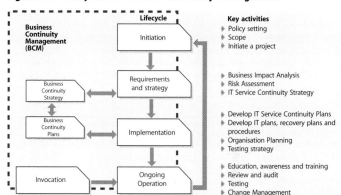

The initiation and requirements stages are principally BCM activities. ITSCM should only be involved in these stages to support the BCM activities and to understand the relationship between the business processes and the impacts of the loss of IT service on these processes. As a result of these initial BIA and Risk Analysis activities, BCM should produce a Business Continuity Strategy. Once this has been done, and the role of IT services within the strategy has been determined, the first real ITSCM task is to produce an ITSCM strategy that underpins the BCM strategy and its needs.

Stage 1 – Initiation

The initiation process covers the whole of the organization and consists of the following activities:

■ **Policy setting** – this should be established and communicated as soon as possible so that all the members of the organization are aware of their responsibilities to comply with and support ITSCM

- **Specify terms of reference and scope** – this includes defining the scope and responsibilities of all staff in the organization. It covers undertaking a Risk Analysis and BIA and determination of the command and control structure required to support a business interruption
- **Allocate resources** – the establishment of an effective Business Continuity and ITSCM environment requires considerable financial and human resources
- **Define the project organization and control structure** – ITSCM and BCM projects are potentially complex and must be well organized and controlled
- **Agree project and quality plans** – plans enable the project to be controlled and variances addressed. Quality plans ensure that the deliverables are achieved to an acceptable level of quality.

Stage 2 – Requirements and strategy

Ascertaining the business requirements for IT service continuity is a critical component of the process of determining how well an organization will survive a business interruption or disaster and the costs that will be incurred. If the requirements analysis is incorrect, or key information has been missed, this could have serious consequences on the effectiveness of ITSCM mechanisms. The requirements analysis is dependent on information from:

- **Requirements, BIA** – the purpose of a BIA is to quantify the impact of the loss of service on the business. This impact could be a 'hard' impact that can be precisely identified, such as financial loss, or a 'soft' impact, such as public relations, morale, health and safety, or loss of competitive advantage. The BIA will identify the most important services to the organization and will therefore be a key input to the strategy. The emphasis should be on more preventive measures for processes and services with earlier and higher impacts, and on continuity and recovery measures for those on which the impact is lower and takes longer to develop. A balanced approach including both measures should be adopted for those in between

- **Requirements, Risk Analysis** – the second driver in determining ITSCM requirements is the likelihood that a disaster or other serious service disruption will occur. This is an assessment of the level of threat and the extent to which an organization is vulnerable to that threat. A Risk Analysis is the assessment of the risks that may give rise to service disruption or security violation. Risk management is concerned with identifying appropriate risk responses or cost-justifiable countermeasures to combat those risks

- **IT Service Continuity Strategy** – the results of the BIA and the Risk Analysis will enable appropriate Business and IT Service Continuity strategies to be produced, in line with the business needs. The ITCSM strategy will be an optimum balance of risk reduction and recovery or continuity options. This includes consideration of the relative service recovery priorities and the changes in relative service priority for the time of day, day of the week, and monthly and annual variations

- **Risk response measures** – most organizations will have to adopt a balanced approach where risk reduction and recovery are complementary and both are required. This entails reducing, as far as possible, the risks to the continued provision of IT. However well planned, it is impossible to completely eliminate all the risks, and therefore recovery options must also be considered

- **ITSCM recovery options** – an organization's ITSCM strategy is a balance between the cost of risk reduction measures and recovery options to support the recovery of critical business processes within agreed timescales. The potential IT recovery options that could to be considered are:

    - **Manual workarounds**: for certain types of services, manual workarounds can be an effective recovery option
    - **Reciprocal arrangements**: in the past, reciprocal arrangements were typical contingency measures where agreements were put in place with another organization using similar technology. This is no longer effective for most IT systems, but can be used for the off-site storage of backups

- **Gradual recovery (Cold Standby)**: this option includes provision of empty accommodation that is fully equipped with power, environmental and local network cabling infrastructure and telecommunications connections. All these are required in a disaster situation for an organization to install its own computer equipment. This may be provided internally or externally and can be fixed or portable
- **Intermediate recovery (Warm Standby)**: this option is selected by organizations that need to recover IT facilities within a predetermined time to prevent impacts to the business process. Most common is the use of commercial facilities offered by third-party recovery organizations to a number of subscribers, spreading the cost across those subscribers. These commercial facilities often include operation, management and support. Commercial recovery services can be provided in self-contained, portable or mobile form where an agreed system is provided within an agreed time
- **Fast recovery (Hot Standby)**: this option provides for fast recovery and restoration of services. Where fast restoration of a service is needed, space can be obtained at a recovery site and systems installed with application systems and communications available, and data mirrored from the operational servers. In the event of a system failure, the customers can then switch over to the backup facility with little loss of service. This facility can be provided internally or externally
- **Immediate recovery** (often referred to as 'hot standby', 'mirroring', 'load balancing' or 'split site'): this option provides for immediate restoration of services, with no loss of service. For business critical services, organizations requiring continuous operation will provide their own facilities within the organization, but not on the same site as the normal operations. Sufficient IT equipment will be 'dual located' in either an owned or a hosted location to run the service, with no loss of service to the customer.

Stage 3 – Implementation

Once the ITSCM strategy has been approved, the IT SCPs need to be produced in line with the Business Continuity Plans (BCPs). ITSCM plans contain the necessary information for critical systems, services and facilities to either continue to be provided or to be reinstated within an acceptable period to the business. Generally, the BCPs rely on the availability of IT services, facilities and resources.

It should be noted that continuity plans are more than just recovery plans, and should include documentation of the resilience measures and the measures that have been put into place to enable recovery, together with explanations of why a particular approach has been taken. However, the format of the plan should allow rapid access to the recovery information itself, perhaps as an appendix that can be accessed directly. All key staff should have access to copies of all the necessary recovery documentation. Management of the distribution of the plans is important to ensure that copies are available to key staff at all times. The plans should be controlled documents (with documents maintained under Change Management). The plan should ensure that all details regarding recovery of the IT services following a disaster are fully documented.

In addition, plans that will also need to be integrated with the main BCP are:

- **Emergency Response Plan** – to interface to all emergency services and activities
- **Damage Assessment Plan** – containing details of damage assessment contacts, processes and plans
- **Salvage Plan** – containing information on salvage contacts, activities and processes
- **Vital Records Plan** – containing details of all vital records and information, together with their location
- **Crisis Management and Public Relations Plan** – the plans on the command and control of crisis situations and management of the media and public relations

- **Accommodation and Services Plan** – detailing the management of facilities and services
- **Security Plan** – showing how all aspects of security will be managed on all sites
- **Personnel Plan** – containing details of how all personnel issues will be managed
- **Communication Plan** – showing how all aspects of communication will be handled and managed
- **Finance and Administration Plan** – detailing emergency authorization and access to essential funds.

Stage 4 – Ongoing operation

This stage consists of the following:

- **Education, awareness and training** – this ensures that all staff are aware of the implications of business continuity and service continuity and consider these as part of their normal working
- **Review** – review of all of the deliverables from the ITSCM process to ensure they remain current
- **Testing** – after initial testing, regular testing should be completed at least annually and after every major business change
- **Change Management** – the Change Management process should ensure that all changes are assessed for their potential impact on the ITSCM plans.

Invocation

Invocation is the ultimate test of the Business Continuity and ITSCM Plans. If all the preparatory work has been successfully completed, and plans developed and tested, then an invocation of the BCPs should be a straightforward process. It is important that due consideration is also given to the design of all invocation processes and the decision to invoke. The decision to invoke must be made quickly, as there may be a lead-time involved in establishing facilities at a recovery site.

The ITSCM process characteristics

Many events may trigger ITSCM activity. These include:

- New or changed business needs, or new or changed services
- New or changed targets within agreements, such as SLRs, SLAs, OLAs or contracts
- The occurrence of a major Incident that requires assessment for potential invocation
- Periodic activities such as the BIA or Risk Analysis activities and maintenance of Continuity Plans
- Assessment of changes and attendance at Change Advisory Board meetings
- Review and revision of business and IT plans and strategies
- Review and revision of designs and strategies
- Recognition or notification of a change of risk or impact of a business process or VBF
- Initiation of tests of continuity and recovery plans.

There are many sources of input required by the ITSCM process:

- Business information – from the organization's business strategy, plans and financial plans
- IT information – from the IT strategy and plans and current budgets
- A Business Continuity Strategy and a set of BCPs
- Service information – SLAs, SLRs, OLAs and contracts from the SLM process
- Financial information – the cost of service provision, the cost of resources and components
- Change information – the Change Schedule from Change Management
- CMS – the relationships between the business, the services, the supporting technology
- BCM and AM testing schedules
- IT SCPs and test reports from supplier and partners, where appropriate.

The outputs from the ITSCM process include:

- A revised ITSCM policy and strategy
- A set of ITSCM plans, together with a set of supporting plans and contracts for recovery services
- BIA exercises and reports, in conjunction with BCM and the business
- Risk Analysis and Management reviews and reports, in conjunction with the business
- An ITSCM testing schedule
- ITSCM test scenarios
- ITSCM test reports and reviews.

Forecasts and predictive reports are used by all areas to analyse, predict and forecast particular business and IT scenarios and their potential solutions.

Many CSFs and KPIs can be used to measure the effectiveness and efficiency of ITSCM, including:

- ITSCM test reports and reviews:
  - All service recovery targets are agreed and documented in SLAs and are achievable within the ITSCM plans
  - Regular and comprehensive testing of ITSCM plans
  - Regular reviews are undertaken, at least annually, of the business and IT continuity plans
  - Overall reduction in the risk and impact of possible failure of IT services
- Awareness throughout the organizations of the plans:
  - Ensure awareness of business impact, needs and requirements throughout IT
  - Ensure that all IT service areas and staff are prepared and able to respond to an invocation of the ITSCM plans
  - Regular communication of the ITSCM objectives and responsibilities within the appropriate business and IT service areas.

ITSCM needs to store the information necessary to maintain a comprehensive set of ITSCM plans. This includes:

- Information from the latest version of the BIA
- Information on risk within a Risk Register, including risk assessment and risk responses
- The latest version of the BCM strategy and BCPs
- Details relating to all completed tests and a schedule of all planned tests
- Details of all ITSCM plans and their contents
- Details of all other plans associated with ITSCM plans
- Details of all existing recovery facilities, recovery suppliers and partners and recovery contracts
- Details of all backup and recovery processes, schedules, systems and media, and their locations.

One of the major challenges facing ITSCM is to provide appropriate plans when there is no BCM process. In this situation, IT is likely to make incorrect assumptions about the criticality of business processes and therefore adopt the wrong continuity strategies and options. Without BCM, expensive ITSCM solutions and plans will be rendered useless by the absence of corresponding plans and arrangements within the business. When there is a BCM process in place, the challenge becomes one of alignment and integration.

Some of the major risks associated with ITSCM include:

- Lack of commitment from the business to the ITSCM processes and procedures
- Lack of commitment from the business and information on future plans and strategies
- Lack of senior management commitment or lack of resources, processes or budget
- The processes focus too much on technology issues and not enough on the business and services

- Risk Analysis and Management are conducted in isolation, not in conjunction with other processes
- ITSCM plans and information become out of date and lose alignment with the business and BCM.

3.7.6   Information Security Management

The goal of the ISM process is to align IT security with business security and ensure that information security is effectively managed in all service and Service Management activities.

Information security is a management activity within the corporate governance framework, and provides the strategic direction for security activities and ensures objectives are achieved. It also ensures that information security risks are appropriately managed and that enterprise information resources are used responsibly. The purpose of ISM is to provide a focus for all aspects of IT security activities.

The objective of information security is to protect the interests of those relying on information, and the systems and communications that deliver the information from harm resulting from failures of availability, confidentiality and integrity. For most organizations, the security objective is met when:

- Information is available and usable when required, and the systems that provide it can appropriately resist attacks and recover from or prevent failures (availability)
- Information is observed by or is disclosed only to those who have a right to know (confidentiality)
- Information is complete, accurate and protected against unauthorized modification (integrity)
- Business transactions, as well as information exchanges between enterprises, or with partners, can be trusted (authenticity and non-repudiation).

Prioritization of confidentiality, integrity and availability must be considered in the context of business and business processes. The primary guide to defining what must be protected and the level of protection required has to come from the business. To be effective, security must address entire business processes from end to end and cover the physical and technical aspects. The ISM process should be the focal point for all IT security issues, and must ensure that an Information Security Policy is produced, maintained and enforced, covering the use and misuse of all IT systems and services. ISM needs to understand the total IT and business security environment, including the:

- Business Security Policy and plans
- Current business operation and its security requirements
- Future business plans and requirements
- Legislative requirements
- Obligations and responsibilities with regard to security contained within SLAs
- The business and IT risks and their management.

Understanding all of this will enable ISM to ensure that all the current and future security aspects and risks of the business are managed cost-effectively. The ISM process should include:

- Enforcement of an Information Security Policy and supporting security policies
- Understanding the agreed current and future security requirements of the business
- An Information Security Management System (ISMS), with supporting processes
- A communications strategy and plan for security, closely linked to business objectives and plans
- A set of security controls that support the Information Security Policy
- An effective security organizational structure
- Documentation of security controls, together with operation and maintenance of controls and risks

- Management of suppliers and contracts regarding access to systems and services
- Monitoring processes to ensure compliance and management of security risks
- Management of all security breaches and Incidents associated with all systems and services
- The proactive improvement of security controls, and security risk management
- Integration of security aspects within all other ITSCM processes.

To achieve effective information security governance, management must establish and maintain an ISMS to guide the development and management of a comprehensive information security programme that supports the business objectives. ISM ensures that an Information Security Policy is maintained and enforced, which fulfils the needs of the Business Security Policy and the requirements of corporate governance. ISM raises awareness of the need for security within all IT services and assets throughout the organization, ensuring that the policy is appropriate for the needs of the organization. ISM manages all aspects of information security within all areas of IT and Service Management activity. It provides assurance of business processes by enforcing appropriate security controls in all areas of IT. ISM achieves this by managing IT risk within business and corporate risk management processes and guidelines.

ISO/IEC 27001 is the formal standard against which organizations may seek independent certification of their ISMS. The ISMS shown in Figure 3.22 illustrates an approach that is widely used and is based on the advice and guidance described in many sources, including ISO/IEC 27001.

Figure 3.22 Framework for managing IT security

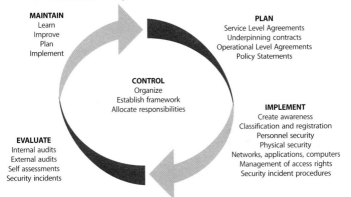

Customers – Requirements – Business Needs

MAINTAIN
Learn
Improve
Plan
Implement

PLAN
Service Level Agreements
Underpinning contracts
Operational Level Agreements
Policy Statements

CONTROL
Organize
Establish framework
Allocate responsibilities

IMPLEMENT
Create awareness
Classification and registration
Personnel security
Physical security
Networks, applications, computers
Management of access rights
Security incident procedures

EVALUATE
Internal audits
External audits
Self assessments
Security incidents

The objectives of the five elements within the framework shown in Figure 3.22 are as follows:

- **Control** – to establish a management framework to initiate and manage information security in the organization, implement the Information Security Policy and control roles and documentation
- **Plan** – to devise and recommend the appropriate security measures, based on an understanding of the requirements of the organization
- **Implement** – to ensure that appropriate procedures, tools and controls are in place to underpin the Information Security Policy
- **Evaluate** – to supervise and check compliance with the security policy by carrying out regular audits, and providing information to external auditors, when required
- **Maintain** – to improve security agreements as specified in, for example, SLAs and OLAs and improve security measures and controls.

The key activities within the ISM process are:

- Production and management of an overall Information Security Policy and a set of policies
- Communication, implementation and enforcement of the security policies and strategy
- Assessment and classification of all information assets and documentation
- Implementation, revision and improvement of a set of security controls and risk assessment
- Monitoring and management of all security breaches and major security Incidents
- Analysis, reporting and reduction of the volumes and impact of security breaches and Incidents
- Schedule and completion of security reviews, audits and penetration tests.

The developed ISM processes, together with the methods, tools and techniques, constitute the security strategy. The security manager should ensure that technologies, products and services are in place and that the overall policy is developed and well published. The security manager is also responsible for security architecture, authentication, authorization, administration and recovery. The security strategy also needs to consider how it will embed good security practices into every area of the business.

Security controls

The Information Security Manager must understand that security is not a step in the lifecycle of services and systems, and that security cannot be solved through technology. Rather, information security must be an integral part of all services and systems and is an ongoing process that needs to be continuously managed using a set of security controls (Figure 3.23).

Figure 3.23 Security controls for threats and Incidents

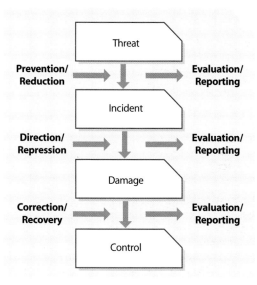

The set of security controls should be designed to support and enforce the Information Security Policy and to minimize all recognized and identified threats. The controls will be considerably more cost-effective if included within the design of all services, including:

- **Preventive** – security measures are used to prevent a security Incident from occurring
- **Reductive** – further measures taken in advance to minimize any possible damage that may occur
- **Detective** – if a security Incident occurs, it is important to discover it as soon as possible

- **Repressive** – measures are then used to counteract any continuation or repetition of the Incident
- **Corrective** – the damage is repaired as far as possible using corrective measures.

The documentation of all controls should be maintained to reflect accurately their maintenance and method of operation.

Management of security breaches and Incidents

In the case of serious security breaches or Incidents, an evaluation is necessary in due course, to determine what went wrong, what caused the security breach or Incident and how it can be prevented in the future. However, this process should not be limited to serious security Incidents. All breaches of security and security Incidents need to be studied in order to gain a full picture of the effectiveness of the security measures as a whole. A reporting procedure for security Incidents is required to be able to evaluate the effectiveness and efficiency of the present security measures based on an insight into all security Incidents.

ISM process characteristics

ISM activity can be triggered by many events. These include:

- New or changed corporate governance guidelines
- New or changed Business Security Policy
- New or changed corporate risk management processes and guidelines
- New or changed business needs or new or changed services
- New or changed requirements within agreements, such as SLRs, SLAs, OLAs or contracts
- Review and revision of business and IT plans and strategies
- Review and revision of designs and strategies
- Service or component security breaches or warnings, events and alerts
- Periodic activities, such as reviewing, revising or reporting, including ISM policies and plans

- Recognition or notification of a change of risk or impact of a business process or VBF
- Requests from other areas, particularly SLM for assistance with security issues.

ISM requires input from many areas, including:

- Business information – from the organization's business strategy, plans and financial plans
- Governance and business security policies and guidelines, security plans and Risk Analysis
- IT information – from the IT strategy and plans and current budgets
- Service information – SLAs, SLRs, OLAs and contracts with details from the Service Portfolio
- Risk Analysis processes and reports – from ISM, AM and ITSCM
- Details of all security events and breaches – from all areas
- Change information – the Change Schedule from Change Management
- CMS – with relationships between the business, services, supporting services and technology
- Details of partner and supplier access – on external access to services and systems.

The outputs produced by the ISM process are used in all areas and should include:

- An overall Information Security Management Policy, together with a set of specific policies
- A Security Management Information System (SMIS), containing information relating to ISM
- Revised security risk assessment processes and reports
- A set of security controls, together with details of the operation, maintenance and associated risks
- Security audits and audit reports
- Security test schedules and plans, including security penetration tests and other security tests
- A set of security classifications and a set of classified information assets

- Reviews and reports of security breaches and major Incidents
- Policies, processes and procedures for managing partners and suppliers and their access.

Many CSFs, KPIs and metrics can be used to assess the effectiveness and efficiency of the ISM process and activities. These metrics need to be developed from the service, customer and business perspective:

- Business protected against security violations:
  - Percentage decrease in security breaches reported to the Service Desk
  - Percentage decrease in the impact of security breaches and Incidents
  - Percentage increase in SLA conformance to security clauses
- The determination of a clear and agreed policy, integrated with the needs of the business:
  - Decrease in the number of non-conformances of the ISM process
- Security procedures that are justified, appropriate and supported by senior management:
  - Increase in the acceptance and conformance of security procedures
  - Increased support and commitment of senior management
- A mechanism for improvement:
  - The number of suggested improvements to security procedures and controls
  - Decrease in the number of security non-conformance events detected during audits and security testing
- Information security is an integral part of all IT services and all ITSM processes:
  - Increase in the number of services and processes conformant with security procedures and controls
- Effective marketing and education in security requirements, IT staff awareness:
  - Increased awareness of the security policy and its contents, throughout the organization
  - Service Desk supporting all services.

Areas of major risks associated with ISM include:

■ Lack of commitment from the business and lack of appropriate information on future activities

■ Lack of senior management commitment or lack of resources and/or budget for the ISM process

■ Too much focus on the technology issues and not enough on the business and service needs

■ Risk activities being conducted in isolation, and not with AM and ITSCM

■ ISM policies, plans and risks becoming out of date and lose alignment with the business.

3.7.7 Supplier Management

The Supplier Management process ensures that suppliers and the services they provide are managed to support IT service targets and business expectations. The aim of this section is to raise awareness of the business context of working with partners and suppliers, and how this work can best be directed towards realizing business benefit for the organization.

The goal of the Supplier Management process is to manage suppliers and the services they supply, to provide seamless quality of IT service to the business, ensuring value for money is obtained.

It is essential that Supplier Management processes and planning are involved in all stages of the Service Lifecycle, from strategy and design, through transition and operation, to improvement. The complex business demands require the complete breadth of skills and capability to support provision of a comprehensive set of IT services to a business; thus the use of value networks and the suppliers and the services they provide are an integral part of any end-to-end solution. Suppliers and the management of suppliers and partners are essential to the provision of quality IT services.

The main objectives of the Supplier Management process are to:

- Obtain value for money from supplier and contracts
- Ensure that underpinning contracts and agreements with suppliers are aligned to business needs
- Manage relationships with suppliers
- Manage supplier performance
- Negotiate and agree contracts with suppliers and manage them through their lifecycle
- Maintain a supplier policy and a supporting Supplier and Contract Database (SCD).

Each service provider should have formal processes for the management of all suppliers and contracts. However, the processes should adapt to cater for the importance of the supplier and/or the contract and the potential business impact on the provision of services. Many suppliers provide support services and products that independently have a relatively minor, and fairly indirect, role in value generation, but collectively make a direct and important contribution to value generation and the implementation of the overall business strategy. The greater the contribution the supplier makes to business value, the more effort the service provider should put into the management of the supplier and the more that supplier should be involved in the development and realization of the business strategy.

The Supplier Management process should include:

- Implementation and enforcement of the supplier policy
- Maintenance of an SCD
- Supplier and contract categorization and risk assessment
- Supplier and contract evaluation and selection
- Development, negotiation and agreement of contracts
- Contract review, renewal and termination
- Management of suppliers and supplier performance
- Agreement and implementation of service and supplier improvement plans
- Maintenance of standard contracts, terms and conditions

- Management of contractual dispute resolution
- Management of sub-contracted suppliers.

Supplier Management often has to comply with organizational or corporate standards, guidelines and requirements, particularly those of corporate legal, finance and purchasing (Figure 3.24).

Figure 3.24 Supplier Management – roles and interfaces

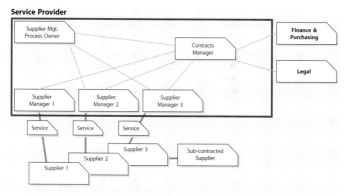

In order to ensure that suppliers provide value for money and meet their service targets, the relationship with each supplier should be owned by an individual within the service provider organization although a single individual may own the relationship for one or many suppliers. To ensure that relationships are developed in a consistent manner and that supplier performance is appropriately reviewed and managed, roles need to be established for a Supplier Management process owner and a Contracts Manager.

The Supplier Management process should align with all corporate requirements and the requirements of all other IT and Service Management processes, particularly ISM and ITSCM. The Supplier Management process attempts to ensure that suppliers meet the terms, conditions and targets of their contracts and agreements, whilst trying to increase the value for money obtained from suppliers and the services they provide. All Supplier Management process activity should be driven by a supplier strategy and policy from Service Strategy. In order to achieve consistency and effectiveness in the implementation of the policy, an SCD should be established, with clearly defined roles and responsibilities (Figure 3.25).

Figure 3.25 Supplier Management process

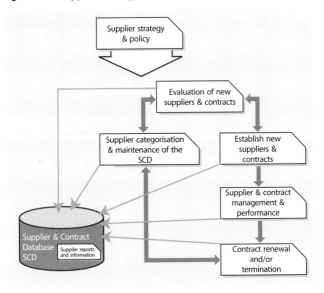

Ideally, the SCD should form an integrated element of a comprehensive CMS or SKMS, recording all supplier and contract details, together with details of the type of service(s) or product(s) provided by each supplier, and all other information and relationships. The services provided by suppliers will also form a key part of the Service Portfolio and the Service Catalogue. The relationship between the supporting services and the IT and business services they support are key to providing quality services. When dealing with external suppliers, it is strongly recommended that a formal contract with clearly defined, agreed and documented responsibilities and targets is established and managed through the stages of the contract lifecycle, from the identification of the business need to its operation and termination.

Supplier Management process characteristics

Supplier Management activity can be triggered by many events. These include:

- New or changed corporate governance guidelines
- New or changed business and IT strategies, policies or plans
- New or changed business needs or new or changed services
- New or changed requirements within agreements, such as SLRs, SLAs, OLAs or contracts
- Review and revision of designs and strategies
- Reviewing or reporting, including review and revision of Supplier Management policies and plans
- Requests from other areas, particularly SLM and Security Management, for assistance with supplier issues
- Requirements for new contracts, contract renewal or contract termination
- Re-categorization of suppliers and/or contracts.

The Supplier Management process will require inputs including:

- **Business information** – from the organization's business strategy, plans and financial plans

- **Supplier and contracts strategy** – this covers the sourcing policy of the service provider
- **Supplier plans and strategies** – details of the business plans and strategies of suppliers
- **Supplier contracts, agreements and targets** – of both existing and new agreements from suppliers
- **Supplier and contract performance information** – of both existing and new contracts and suppliers
- **IT information** – from the IT strategy and plans and current budgets
- **Performance issues**: Incidents and Problems relating to poor contract or supplier performance
- **Financial information** – from Financial Management, the cost of supplier service(s) and contracts
- **Service information** – from the SLM process, with details of the services and service quality
- **CMS** – information on the relationships between the business, services and technology.

The outputs of Supplier Management are used within all other parts of the process, by many other processes and by other parts of the organization. These include:

- **The SCD** – Supplier Management and contract information
- **Supplier and contract performance information and reports** – used as input to review meetings
- **Supplier and contract review meeting minutes** – produced to record the minutes and actions
- **Supplier SIPs** – used to record all improvement actions and plans
- **Supplier survey reports** – feedback from individuals should be collated to ensure quality of service.

Many CSFs, KPIs and metrics can be used to assess the effectiveness and efficiency of the Supplier Management process and activities:

- Business protected from poor supplier performance or disruption:
  - Increase in the number of suppliers meeting the targets within the contract
  - Reduction in the number of breaches of contractual targets
- Supporting services and their targets align with business needs and targets:
  - Increase in the number of service and contractual reviews held with suppliers
  - Increase in the number of supplier and contractual targets aligned with SLAs and SLRs
- Availability of services is not compromised by supplier performance:
  - Reduction in the number of service breaches caused by suppliers
  - Reduction in the number of threatened service breaches caused by suppliers
- Clear ownership and awareness of supplier and contractual issues:
  - Increase in the number of suppliers with nominated supplier managers
  - Increase in the number of contracts with nominated contract managers.

All the information required by Supplier Management should be contained within the SCD. This should include all information relating to suppliers and contracts, as well as all the information relating to the operation of the supporting services provided by suppliers. This information should be integrated and maintained in alignment with all management systems, particularly the Service Portfolio and CMS.

Supplier Management faces many challenges, such as:

- Continually changing business and IT needs, managing change in parallel with delivering service
- Working with an imposed non-ideal contract, a contract that has poor targets or conditions
- Legacy issues, especially with services recently outsourced
- Insufficient expertise retained within the organization
- Being tied into long-term contracts, with no possibility of improvement
- Situations where the supplier depends on the organization in fulfilling the service delivery
- Disputes over charges
- Interference by either party in the running of the other's operation
- Being caught in a daily fire-fighting mode, losing the proactive approach
- Communication – not interacting often enough or quick enough or focusing on the right issues
- Personality conflicts
- One party using the contract to the detriment of the other party
- Losing the strategic perspective, focusing on operational issues.

Key elements that can help to avoid the above issues are:

- Clearly written, well-defined and well-managed contracts
- Mutually beneficial relationships
- Clearly defined (and communicated) roles and responsibilities on both sides
- Good interfaces and communications between the parties
- Well-defined Service Management processes on both sides
- Selecting suppliers who have achieved certification against international quality standards.

The major areas of risk associated with Supplier Management include:

- Lack of commitment from the business and senior management to Supplier Management
- Lack of appropriate information on future business and IT policies, plans and strategies
- Lack of resources and/or budget for the Supplier Management process
- Legacy of badly written and agreed contracts that do not underpin or support business needs
- Suppliers fail or are incapable of meeting the targets or terms and conditions of the contract
- Supplier personnel or organizational culture are not aligned to that of the service provider
- Suppliers are not cooperative and are not willing to take part in or support the required processes
- Suppliers are taken over and relationships, personnel and contracts are changed
- The demands of corporate supplier and contract procedures are excessive and bureaucratic
- Poor corporate financial processes, such as procurement and purchasing.

3.8   SERVICE DESIGN TECHNOLOGY-RELATED ACTIVITIES

This section considers the technology-related activities of requirements engineering and the development of technology architectures. The technology architectures covers Infrastructure, Environmental, Data/Information and Application Management.

3.8.1   Requirements engineering

Requirements engineering is the approach by which sufficient rigour is introduced into the process of understanding and documenting the business and user's requirements, and ensuring traceability of changes to each requirement. This process comprises the stages of elicitation, analysis (which feeds back into the elicitation) and validation. All these contribute to the production of a rigorous, complete requirements document. The core of this document is a repository of individual requirements that are developed and managed. Often these requirements are instigated by IT but ultimately they need to be documented and agreed with the business.

A fundamental assumption here is that the analysis of the current and required business processes results in functional requirements met through IT services (comprising applications, data, infrastructure, environment and support skills).

The management and operational requirements can be used to prescribe the quality attributes of the application being built. These quality attributes can be used to design test plans for testing the applications on the compliance to management and operational requirements.

Users have formally defined roles and activities as user representatives in requirements definition and acceptance testing. They should be actively involved in identifying all aspects of service requirements.

3.8.2 Data Management

One way of improving the quality of data is to use a Data Management process that establishes policy and standards, provides expertise and makes it easier to handle the data aspects of new services. This should then allow full Data/Information Asset Management to add value to the services delivered, reduce business risks, reduce costs and stimulate innovation with business processes.

Four areas of management are included within the scope of Data/ Information Management:

■ **Management of data resources** – the governance of information in the organization must ensure that all these resources are known and that responsibilities have been assigned for their management

- **Management of data/information technology** – the management of the IT that underpins the organization's information systems
- **Management of information processes** – the process of managing data/information through the lifecycle
- **Management of data standards and policies** – the organization will need to define standards and policies for its Data Management as an element of an IT strategy.

The team supporting the Data Management process may also provide a business information support service. In this case, the team is able to answer questions about the meaning, format and availability of data internal to the organization, because it manages the metadata. It can also understand and explain what external data might be needed in order to carry out necessary business processes and will take the necessary action to source this.

During requirements and initial design, Data Management can assist design and development teams with service-specific data modelling and give advice on the use of various techniques to model data. During detailed ('physical') design and development, the Data Management function can provide technical expertise on database management systems (DBMSs) and on how to convert initial 'logical' models of data into physical, product specific, implementations.

Data is an asset and has value. It is more common to value data in terms of what it is worth to the owner organization. Data can be initially classified as operational, tactical or strategic, depending on its content and use. An alternative method is to use a security classification of data and documents. This is usually adopted as a corporate policy within an organization.

Data management can assist the service developer by making sure responsibilities for data ownership are taken seriously by the business and by the IT department. One of the most successful ways of doing this is to get the business and the IT department to sign up to a data charter – a set of procedural standards and guidance for the careful management of data in the organization, by adherence to corporately defined standards. These should cover the data and its migration, storage, capture, retrieval, usage, integrity and other related issues.

3.8.3 Applications Management

Applications, along with data and infrastructure components such as hardware, the operating system and middleware, make up the technology components that are part of an IT service. The application itself is only one component, albeit an important one of the service. Therefore, it is important that the application delivered matches the agreed requirements of the business. However, many organizations spend too much time focusing on the functional requirements of the new service and application, and insufficient time is spent designing the management and operational requirements (non-functional requirements) of the service. This means that when the service becomes operational, it meets all of the functionality required, but it totally fails to meet the expectation of the business and the customers in terms of its quality and performance; therefore, it becomes unusable.

Two alternative approaches are necessary to fully implement Application Management. One approach employs an extended Service Development Lifecycle (SDLC) to support the development of an IT service. The other approach takes a global view of all services to ensure the ongoing maintainability and manageability of the applications.

The Application Portfolio is simply a full record of all applications within the organization and is dynamic in its content. Some organizations maintain a separate Application Portfolio with separate attributes, whereas in other organizations the Application Portfolio is stored within the CMS, together with the appropriate relationships. Some organizations combine the Application Portfolio with the Service Portfolio. It is for each organization to decide the most appropriate strategy for its own needs. What is clear is that there should be very close relationships and links between the applications and the services they support and the infrastructure components used.

The concept of an application framework is a powerful one. The application framework covers all management and operational aspects and actually provides solutions for all the management and operational requirements that surround an application. Utilizing the concept of an application framework, the first step of the application design phase is to identify the appropriate application framework. If the application framework is mature, a large number of the design decisions are given. If it is not mature, and all management and operational requirements cannot be met on top of an existing application framework, the preferred strategy is to collect and analyse the requirements that cannot be dealt with in the current version of the application framework. Based on the application requirements, new requirements can be defined for the application framework. Next, the application framework can be modified so that it can cope with the application requirements. In fact, the whole family of applications that corresponds to the application framework can then use the newly added or changed framework features.

3.9   TECHNOLOGY CONSIDERATIONS

It is generally recognized that the use of Service Management tools is essential for the success of all but the very smallest process implementations. However, it is important that the tool being used supports the processes – not the other way around. As a general rule, processes should not be modified to fit the tool. However, with the use of tools to support processes, there is a need to be pragmatic and recognize that there may not be a tool that supports the designed process totally, so an element of process redesign may be necessary. Do not limit the requirements to functionality: consider the product's ability to perform, enlarge the size of the databases, recover from failure and maintain data integrity. Does the product conform to international standards? Is it efficient enough to enable you to meet your Service Management Requirements?

3.9.1 Service Design tools

Many tools and techniques can be used to assist with the design of services and their associated components, covering all aspects of design. These include both proprietary and non-proprietary tools. They can assist design processes and ensure that standards and conventions are followed. Development of Service Designs can be simplified by the use of tools that provide graphical views of the service and its constituent components, from the business processes, through the service and SLA to the infrastructure, environment, data and applications, processes, OLAs, teams, contracts and suppliers. Some Configuration Management tools provide such facilities, and are sometimes referred to as an element of BSM tools. Configuration Management tools can contain or be linked to 'auto-discovery' tools and mechanisms and allow the relationships between all of these elements to be graphically represented, thus providing the ability to drill down within each component and obtaining detailed information if needed.

These types of tool not only facilitate the design processes, but also greatly support and assist all stages in the Service Lifecycle, including:

- All aspects of the service and its management through all stages of the Service Lifecycle
- Service achievement, SLA, OLA, contract and supplier measurement and management
- Consolidated metrics with views from management dashboards down to component information
- Consistent and consolidated views across all processes, systems, technologies and groups
- Relationships and integration of the business and its processes with IT services and processes
- Comprehensive analysis facilities, enabling informed decision-making

- Management of service costs, relationships, interfaces and interdependencies
- Management of the Service Portfolio and Service Catalogue, CMS and the SKMS.

3.9.2 Service Management tools

Tools will enable the Service Design processes to work more effectively. Tools will increase efficiency and effectiveness, and provide a wealth of management information, leading to the identification of weak areas. The longer-term benefits to be gained from the use of tools are cost savings and increased productivity, which in turn can lead to an increase in the quality of the IT service provision. The use of tools allows centralization of key processes and the automation and integration of core Service Management processes. The raw data collected by the tools can be analysed, resulting in the identification of 'trends'. Preventive measures can then be implemented, again improving the quality of the IT service provision.

Some points that organizations should consider when evaluating Service Management tools are:

- Data structure, data handling and integration
- Integration of multi-vendor infrastructure components, and the need to absorb new components
- Conformity to international open standards
- Flexibility in implementation, usage and data sharing
- Usability – the ease of use permitted by the user interface
- Support for monitoring service levels
- Distributed clients with a centralized shared database (e.g. client server)
- Conversion requirements for previously tracked data
- Data backup, control and security
- Support options provided by the tool vendor
- Scalability at increasing of capacity (the number of users, volume of data and so on).

Consideration must be given to the exact requirements for the tool. What are the mandatory requirements and what are the desired requirements? Generally, the tool should support the processes, not the other way round, so minimize modification of the processes to fit the tool. Where possible, it is better to purchase a fully integrated tool (although not at the expense of efficiency and effectiveness) to underpin many (if not all) Service Management processes. If this is not possible, consideration must be given to the interfaces between the various tools.

3.10 IMPLEMENTING SERVICE DESIGN

This section of the publication considers the task of implementing the Service Design processes and tackles issues such as:

- Where do we start?
- How do we improve?
- How do we know we are making progress?

The process, policy and architecture for the design of IT services outlined in this publication will need to be documented and utilized to ensure the appropriate innovative IT services can be designed and implemented to meet current and future agreed business requirements.

The ITSM processes outlined in this publication and in the other publications in this series will also need to be implemented to ensure service delivery that matches the requirements of the business.

The question often asked is 'Which process shall I implement first?' The real answer is all of them, as the true value of implementing all of the Service Management processes is far greater than the sum of the individual processes. All the processes are interrelated, and in some cases are totally dependent on others. What is ultimately required is a single, integrated set of processes, providing management and control of a set of IT services throughout their entire lifecycle.

While recognizing that, to get the complete benefit of implementing ITSM, all of the processes need to be addressed, it is also recognized that it is unlikely that organizations can do everything at once. It is therefore recommended that the areas of greatest need be addressed first. A detailed assessment should be undertaken to ascertain the strengths and weaknesses of IT service provision. This should include customer satisfaction surveys, talking to customers, talking to IT staff and analysing the processes in action. From this assessment, short-, medium- and long-term strategies can be developed. It may be that 'quick wins' need to be implemented in the short term to improve the current situation, but these improved processes may have to be discarded or amended as part of the medium- or long-term strategies. If 'quick wins' are implemented, it is important that they are not done at the expense of the long-term objectives, so these must be considered at all times

A full description of the Continual Service Improvement (CSI) stage of the ITIL Service Management Lifecycle can be found in both the CSI *Key Element Guide* and the CSI core practice guide.

3.11 KEY MESSAGES

Service Design, as described in this publication, covers the design of appropriate and innovative IT services to meet current and future agreed business requirements. Service Design develops an SDP and looks at selecting the appropriate Service Design model. The various sourcing models available and their respective merits have also been considered.

The publication also discusses the fundamentals of the design processes and the five aspects of the design:

■ The design of service solutions, including the functional requirements, resources and capabilities

■ The design of Service Management systems and tools, especially the Service Portfolio

■ The design of the technology architectures and management systems

- The design of the processes needed to design, transition, operate and improve the services
- The design of the measurement systems, methods and metrics for the services.

The publication has explained that the better and more careful the design, the better the solution taken into live operation. It is also highly likely that with better design, less re-work time will be needed during the transition and live phases.

The scope of this publication includes the design of services, as well as the design of Service Management systems and processes. Service Design is not limited to new services, but includes change necessary to increase or maintain value to customers over the lifecycle of services.

This publication explains that pragmatism sometimes overrides the perfect solution where we know what it would be, but the amount of effort and cost does not justify the perfect solution. As always, the solution will depend on the business needs and the business requirements, and it is imperative that whatever is done within IT has a direct benefit to the overall business.